Horror Stories Of I.R.S. Taxpayer Harassment

Updated and expanded version of

Fairy Tales From The I.R.S.

True Stories taken from my files of dealing with the I.R.S. for over 60 years.

You can't believe what these folks can and will do to harass taxpayers.

Story Written By: Carey Erichson
Illustrations By: Janet Welch

DEDICATION

I would like to dedicate this book to the United States Government and all of its subsidiaries.

This includes the internal revenue service, (no caps in this book, as they are the bad guys), for without them, this book could not have been written.

My sincere thanks to all of my clients and friends who have shared their never ending tax problems with me over the years.

Sometimes we whipped them big, but we always held our own.

WELCOME TO THE WORLD OF TAXATION

Here is the new notice of a tax deficiency sent out by the internal revenue service. As you can see it is a threatening letter to intimidate any and all taxpayers.

The following is an actual notice to one of my clients. This type of letter started some time in 2015 or 2016.

~~~~~~~~~~~

Dear Taxpayer:

We have determined that there is a deficiency (increase) in your income tax as shown for the tax year 2013.

This letter is your NOTICE OF DEFICIENCY, as required by law. The enclosed statement shows how we figured the deficiency.

If you want to contest this determination in court before making any payment, you have until the Last Date to Petion Tax Court (90 days from the date of this letter to file a petition with the United States Tax Court for a re determination of the amount of your tax.

Blah – Blah – Blah -------

If you decide **not** to file a petition with the Tax Court, please sign and return the enclosed waiver form to us. This will permit us to access the deficiency quickly and will limit the accumulation of interest.

Blah – Blah – Blah ------

Now if this type of letter doesn't freak out a normal taxpayer, nothing will. It is intimidation of the highest degree and will scare the recipient taxpayer into paying whether they owe the money or not. This is when you need a good tax adviser.

NO ONE WANTS TO GO TO TAX COURT INCLUDING THE I.R.S !

Here is another new wrinkle the i.r.s. is throwing at taxpayers.

Starting sometime in the year 2017, the i.r.s. will hire outside contractors to collect delinquent tax bills. They are doing this because they are so short of personnel.

Short handed my ass, if ½ of them worked a full 8 hours per day they could fire the other half of their staff. But that will never happen.

Anyway, the i.r.s. has hand picked 4 outstanding collection firms to act as tax collectors for them. I think this is done more to improve their image as it is removing them one step away from interacting with the general public, which they do not do so well.

Here are the 4 handpicked collection agencies:

CBE – Waterloo, IA
ConServe – Fairport, NY
Performant – Pleasanton, CA
Pioneer – Horseheads, NY

So here is how it goes. You will be notified of a tax deficiency by mail. The i.r.s. does not phone tax payers. If the deficiency can not be resolved with in a specified time then your account will be turned over to one of their collection agencies.

Have you ever dealt with a collection agency? Not a pleasant experience. They are nice and helpful for the first one or two phone calls and then their true beast comes out, along with threats and everything else.

Collection agencies only get paid for what they collect and if they do not collect then their cash flow goes to zero. They do not like that.

Since this will be a new experience in the tax world I can not make any comments now, but I'm sure I will have some juicy stories in the years to come.

ABOUT THE AUTHOR

Carey Erichson has been a practicing tax accountant for over 60 years. During this time, he has experienced just about everything one could expect to happen with income taxes and the internal revenue service. (no caps in this book for them)

Along with his tax and accounting practice, Carey has owned and operated at least 27 businesses including restaurants, retail shops, construction, publishing and manufacturing. The world of business has truly fascinated him and he is always in the middle of some business activity.

To complement his accounting practice, Carey became a real estate broker in Nevada, where he specialized in selling businesses.

His hobbies include fishing, golf and bowling. He bowled professionally for over 30 years. His devotion to bowling lead to becoming a highly regarded bowling instructor. He specialized in working with the Junior Bowling Programs throughout the states of California and Nevada.

He has served on the Board of Directors for many corporations and devoted many hours to help the less fortunate find work and a place in life.

Carey Erichson has four patent applications and 34 copyrights to his credit.

As you read this book, you will notice that his well rounded business knowledge and experience has been captured in writing. There is a lot to read between the lines.

PREFACE

Many years ago I heard the old cliche, "The only thing we can be assured of in this life are death and taxes". With this bit of wisdom, I decided to become a tax consultant. If for no other reason, it appeared to offer steady employment.

I have been doing taxes for over 60 years and it seems when April 15th of each year passes, I know less about tax returns today than when I first started. Not only have the tax laws changed, but those silly tax returns get more and more complicated.

This book is inspired by the many experiences of my clients, friends and relatives. Throughout the book, we will be telling little stories about some "screwup" experienced by poor taxpayers over the years.

I am not going to bore you with a bunch of tax laws, as I'm sure you wouldn't understand them, (I sure don't), and I don't want this book to be prescribed as good sleeping material. Taxes are a very important part of our everyday life and to have good financial planning, some understanding of taxes is imperative.

Over the years I have seen so many errors in tax planning and return preparation by attorneys, C.P.A.s and of course, "Ted the Taxman" that I feel a strong need for the average taxpayer to be better educated. A good example would be single parents who have experienced a bad divorce. When they find out the tax consequences of the bad advice they received, or in many cases no advice, my stomach turns from the expressions on their face when they see a large tax bill they can't pay. We will have a chapter on divorces.

Tax audits make for interesting writing. Probably 80% of all taxpayers don't want to know anything about their taxes, but 100% are scared to death about being audited. We will also have a chapter on audits.

Throughout the book we will have some humor and cartoons that may not be appreciated by all of the readers. These are not meant to be sexist or slander anyone, but they seemed to fit the bill at the time of this writing. Some of the humor doesn't even apply to taxes, but like I said earlier, I don't want this book prescribed as good sleeping material.

Carey Erichson

TABLE OF CONTENTS

TAXPAYER'S CONSENSUS
(Glossary of Terms)

Income Taxes = Dirty Word

1040 Pamphlet = Dirty Book

I.R.S. = Epitome of Arrogance

I.R.S. Auditor = Nosy Nincompoop

I.R.S. Audit = Worst Nightmare

Income Tax Laws = Bible Written Backwards

Balance Due = Horror Story

Social Security = Piggy Bank with Hole in Bottom

Estimated Taxes = I.R.S. Honor system

Withholding = Charitable Contributions

W4 Form = Cheat sheet

April 15th = The Real April Fool's Day

THE HAPPY TAXPAYER

THIS PICTURE SAYS IT ALL!!

WHY DO YOU PAY TAXES?
(You haven't read my book yet)

Ladies and gentlemen, if you did not have to file a tax return and pay taxes, I would be out of work and this is a "no-no".

To be a full blooded American citizen, it is very important for you to have a car payment, large credit card balances and some kind of a tax bill. How can we keep the Federal Government in the lifestyle to which they have been accustomed if we do not pay taxes?

Americans complain more about taxes than any country in the world. It may come as a surprise to you, but Americans pay very little taxes compared to other developed nations. Our percentage of tax on income ranks low on an international scale.

What do we get for our tax dollars? Big Fat Cat politicians and a whole bunch of irritating regulations! I bet you thought I was going to say "nothing".

America is a great country. We are the most prosperous, most productive and technologically advanced society on earth. But we are also the nosiest individuals on earth. We put our nose into everyone's business. We even pay other countries so we can muddle in their puddle.

Our politicians are a bunch of little busybody people. They can afford to do this because they have our tax dollars to work with. If our government ever had to turn a profit, you would see the greatest downsizing in American history.

In order to just run the country and pay attention to business, they could cut 80% of the government payroll. This is not possible due to their committee policy. We have committees to watch over committees. When one committee does not perform according to policy, they add another committee to oversee the committee that was overseeing the committee that did not perform up to our policies.

How about the $250,000 toilet seat our government purchased along with the $50,000 hammer? When this was revealed years ago we really added some committees to oversee some committees. The only problem is that we are still paying outrageous prices for some government items. There are some excellent books on the market about our government's purchasing habits. Check the libraries for these books. Very interesting reading.

How about the studies our government sponsors? These are really important to running the country. One study was regarding the sex life of the African firefly, while another was on the eating habits of a desert lizard. Most recently was a study on why welfare mothers continue to have sex and children. I would love to hear the answers to this last one!

One thing I have noticed over the years is the way Republican and Democrat taxpayers look at our taxing system. Without getting into politics, I will briefly summarize the two political factions. Democrats are generally for the working man, while Republicans favor the business owners. Whether this is entirely true or not makes no difference for what you are about to read.

When I interview new tax clients, it is my job to ask a series of personal questions. This is not to be nosy, but to understand their tax situation and tax planning philosophy. Well, you cannot believe some of the topics that come out of what I consider simple questions. (And I never mention politics.)

Right off the top, a Democrat taxpayer will start harping on the Republican factions in our government that favors his boss and gives big tax breaks to the wealthy. On the other side of the coin, we have the Republican taxpayer who starts his own war over the Democrats giving all of his tax money away to the welfare programs.

Now that I know my new client is a Republican or Democrat, I proceed to ask the second question in the interview. It makes no difference which party they may be affiliated with, no one likes taxes. In fact not too many of them like our government. I still don't know how our Presidents get elected because no one seems to like them, either.

I have concluded that between January and April of each year, nobody likes anybody else. Maybe we should switch our income tax deadline to some date between Thanksgiving and Christmas when everyone is in a jolly good mood. It sure would make the tax season a lot more pleasant.

I have learned over the years to agree with my clients right from the start or I would never get to the third and fourth questions in the interview. No matter which party they vote for, my job is to keep the peace at the interview table. So much for politics.

Where do our tax dollars go? I haven't the slightest idea. We have all seen the diagram of the pie and how it is cut up into government spending. The only difference in how the pie is sliced depends on which party is in office. We elect different pie slicers every four years.

The biggest governmental expenditure is interest. We owe so much money that we will never pay off the national debt. This is the government's personal credit card. Just like all of us, they are in way over their heads. Now, the average American citizen puts money into a bank savings account earning 2½% and goes out and racks up expenses on the good old credit card at 18½%. Our government goes out and lends money to all of it's foreign buddies at 2½% and then pays only 8½% on it's credit card. Well, that makes the government 10% smarter than you. How does that make you feel? (I just had to put that in here)!

On many occasions we have all talked about why we cannot get better politicians in Washington, DC. The answer I have always heard is that there is not enough money being paid to our legislators and top brass. I believe the President only makes around $400,000 a year and that is considered peanuts compared to the corporate world. Now, the corporate Presidents have to work hard and turn a profit in at least three of the five proceeding years. Our President of the United States does not have to turn a profit in one out of over 200 years, so why should we pay him a large amount of money?

I would like to be President Of The United States! When was the last time we had an accountant as President? I can slice up a pie as well as the rest of them.

~~~~~~~~~~~~~~~~~~~~~~~~~~~~~~~~~~~

"The Eiffel Tower is the Empire State building
after taxes"   (Quoted by someone)

~~~~~~~~~~~~~~~~~~~~~~~~~~~~~~~~~~~

OUR GOVERNMENT
(i.r.s. DIVISION)

We have had a form of government controlled taxation since the birth of the United States. Taxes in those days were tariffs coming from English law.

As the colonies grew, they became disenchanted with the English tariffs and all other control so they made up their own rules and forms of taxation. The first known personal income tax dates back to 1646 in Massachusetts. This income tax spread to other colonies, but the laws were very weak and there could be no determination of actual income received by tradesman and laborers.

Over the years many methods of taxation were attempted, but again there was little success in standardizing a fair and accepted system.

In 1909, a 1% excise tax was imposed on all corporations having incomes of $5,000 or more. At the same time, Congress proposed an amendment to the Constitution making permissible a tax on all incomes without apportionment among the states according to population.

Known as the 16th Amendment, it was enacted October 3, 1913, and made retroactive to March 1, 1913.

The income tax was born!!!

Now I am only guessing, but I assume some shrewd individual, somewhere, began devising some kind of tax shelter to get out of paying income taxes on October 4, 1913.

Over the years, our system of taxation has become so complex that I doubt if anyone really knows what we have and where we are going with it.

The first problem we have is that laws are not made or passed by the i.r.s.. This is all done in the Houses of Congress. These Houses of Congress are made up mostly of attorneys. We really don't have a second problem, because the first one says it all.

Now attorneys are really nice people at a cocktail party and maybe on the golf course, but give them an inch and you will be walking a mile from there on out. They just don't make sense to the average layman.

Don't get me started on attorneys here, as they are a subject of another whole book I'm going to write.

I think we had better get back to our government and the **area** of taxation. Since October 3, 1913, we have added to the tax code at least 40,000 volumes of paper. The exact count of how large the internal revenue code actually is has been kept a secret from everyone, because no agency wants to be responsible for the mess that has been created.

I don't know why the internal revenue service was created, except for the fact that no elected official wanted to be associated with collecting money and harassing taxpayers so they opened up another division and laid it on them.

The internal revenue service is so fouled up that they have never passed the General Accounting Office's audit that is performed every so many years. They flunked the last audit so badly that it was a complete embarrassment to the acting commissioner. Nothing was in balance and nothing could be accounted for. So many records were lost or as testimony put it, "misplaced", that they canceled the audit for a spell while officials decided what to do.

Every year tax practitioners receive bulletins and newsletters on various i.r.s. activities and problems. Quite a few will be published in this book as little side stories. Some of these stories are really bizarre. I would have a tendency not to believe them, except I have experienced a few of my own.

We all make mistakes, unfortunately more times than we want to admit, but to have a public entity do this over and over without any rhyme or reason is more than most of us can understand.

The worst part of the whole thing is that they get away with it because we, as taxpayers, are afraid to speak up or file legitimate complaints.

The i.r.s. makes more than their share of mistakes. As published in a newsletter, here is a small list of items that will give you an idea of their competence.

1) The i.r.s. could not account for 64% of the items in their own budget.

2) The i.r.s. gave taxpayers the wrong answer to tax questions 8,500,000 times in one year.

3) The i.r.s. sent out over 5,000,000 incorrect tax delinquency notices in one year.

4) The i.r.s. penalized over 3,000,000 women erroneously for getting married or divorced.

5) The i.r.s. spent over 8 billion dollars on a computer system that doesn't work.

The biggest problem with the internal revenue service is that the organization is just too big. I don't know how many employees they have, but my guess would be somewhere around 150,000 to 200,000. If you add the people who actually work, the number would increase by a few thousand more.

~~~~~~~~~~~~~~~~~~~~~~~~~~~~~~~~
"A taxpayer is someone who works for
the federal government but who doesn't
have to take a civil service examination"
(Ronald Reagan)

~~~~~~~~~~~~~~~~~~~~~~~~~~~~~~~~~~

Over the years, I personally have had very few problems with internal revenue personnel. Too many taxpayers get completely irate with i.r.s. personnel and this is wrong. If you do not like the person you are talking with, just ask for another representative.

My standard procedure with i.r.s. employees is that if we are not communicating in the same tone I just ask for their supervisor. This gets me quick answers and puts the idiot in their office at a complete disadvantage because this amounts to a customer complaint.

The most important strategy to follow when working with an i.r.s. agent is to level out the playing field from the first contact on.

One of the biggest inequities in our tax laws, (and this is going to change very soon), is that the taxpayer is presumed guilty until proven innocent. Our courts of law are exactly the opposite as we are innocent until proven guilty.

This puts the taxpayer at a disadvantage before they even start. Due to this inequity, the internal revenue service agents have nothing to gain or lose by being unreasonable. This attitude is rampant throughout the organization. If the computer says you are wrong, then you are wrong and they plan to get you.

A great deal of what we have just discussed will be covered in the area of tax audits. Just remember that when you are talking with a revenue agent it is wise not to play your hand out too early and don't tell them anything that they do not ask for.

~~~~~~~~~~~~~~~~~~~~~~~~~~~~~~~~~~~~~~

All holidays are being switched around this year except one---April Fool's Day. That will still be on April 15th.

~~~~~~~~~~~~~~~~~~~~~~~~~~~~~~~~~~~~~~

TAXES IN GENERAL
(Boring Subject)

Nothing could be more boring than to read a book with a lot of facts and figures. Taxes are very boring so please bear with me as I put a few facts before you.

There are literally hundreds of taxes hidden in all the products we buy, things we do and objects we see. The ones we are concerned with are those we pay directly as taxes.

The four main taxes we pay are:
> Federal & State Income
> Social Security
> Real Estate
> Sales & Use

From random returns in my office, we can conclude in general, that the average income family pays about 30% in taxes. Unfortunately, we can do nothing about taxes we pay except income taxes. Here, with a little bit of tax planning, we can lighten our burden and keep some more money in our jeans.

Taxes to the average worker are all those "funny looking" numbers on the paycheck before you get to the spendable amount.

During the first few months of the year you will mail in a silly, complicated form to the internal revenue service, and wait about six weeks for them to send you another paycheck, (refund), for filing the return and being an honest citizen. So what's the big deal? Well, the big deal is that with a little bit of tax planning you might possibly get a bigger refund.

Proper tax planning begins long before the start of the new tax year. You have to decide just what records are necessary to keep and how much detail and time you are willing to spend to save on tax dollars.

Many people start out the new year with big ideas. They review last year's records, discuss what they want to accomplish and start to keep all kinds of records. But after a few months they become careless and lazy and eventually stop altogether. This usually happens when warm weather and spring fever set in because golf, tennis and gardening are more fun.

For businesses, proper tax planning can save thousands of dollars just by purchasing materials and equipment in one month as opposed to another. For individuals the tax savings are normally less, but just as important for items such as paying medical bills, mortgages (interest), taxes, etc. in December as opposed to January of the following tax year.

Tax Planning Philosophy

"We agree with the board and the taxpayer
that in a transaction, otherwise within an
exception of the tax law, does not lose its
immunity, because it is actuated by a desire
to avoid or, if one choose, to evade, taxation.
Anyone may arrange his affairs that his taxes
shall be as low as possible; he is not bound
to choose the pattern which will best pay the
Treasury"; (Quoting Judge Learned Hand from
Helvering v. Gregory (1934) 69 F. (2d) 809
at 810

I haven't the slightest idea what he said, but the above quotation is one of the most famous and referred to cases in tax law.

Now that you know all about tax planning and the philosophy behind it, we can move right along with a chart to show us all how fortunate we are financially.

TAXPAYER BALANCE OF TRADE

RECEIPTS   100%

EXPENDITURES
Taxes   30%
Mortgages   25%
Food & Clothing   25%
Automobile   12%
Medical and Dental   10%
Fun and Games   15%
Total   117%

DEFICIT BEFORE INFLATION 17%

Do these numbers ring a bell with anyone? (I'm referring to the deficit number). If you think I'm kidding or making up these numbers, take a look at your credit card balances!!

This "heavy stuff" writing is getting to me so I think it's about time for a joke. My publisher says to go easy on jokes, so we will stay with a famous quote.

~~~~~~~~~~~~~~~~~~~~~~~~~~~~~~~~~~~~~~~
"Gone With The Wind is going to be the biggest
flop in the history of Hollywood. I'm just glad
it"ll be Clark Gable who's falling flat on his face
and not Gary Cooper"
Gary Cooper, 1938)
~~~~~~~~~~~~~~~~~~~~~~~~~~~~~~~~~~~~~~~

EVER WONDER WHERE IT GOES?

HORROR STORIES
(The i.r.s. at its best)

Some poor taxpayer had a real trip with the i.r.s. several years ago. John and Mary were married, with children and doing very well for themselves. John was employed as a chemist while Mary was selling real estate as an independent contractor. Each year they filed their taxes, got a refund and never gave this area much thought.

As the years passed, John and Mary got a divorce and went their separate ways. About three years afterwards, Mary got a notice from the i.r.s. stating that she did not file a tax return during the last year she and John were still together.

The notice claimed she earned $30,000 in 1099 income that year, but did not file a tax return. Mary about died! With interest and penalties she was in debt some $8,000 and they were going to attach her wages, bank account and everything else she had.

Mary phoned John and laid the panic button on him. John assured her that the taxes were filed properly and they even got a nice refund that year. Since their prior taxman had passed away, (taxes will do it to you!!), he said he would mail her a copy of the return and for her to take it to her new tax preparer and let him handle the situation.

Mary did as John instructed. The new tax preparer filed all the necessary documents and waited for a response. Well folks, you have to realize that the i.r.s. is in no hurry to respond to anything, and in Mary's case did just that--nothing.

As time passed Mary got another notice and at the same time was informed by her employer that her wages were attached. Next she was informed by the bank that her account was attached and drained of the small amount available. The i.r.s. was doing their thing.

Mary's taxman finally got in touch with someone at the i.r.s. who apparently did not have a fight with their spouse the night before, and was very sympathetic with the situation. The levy was put on hold for nine weeks giving each party time to investigate the situation.

The story goes on about the stress and dismay of Mary, but to get to the heart of the situation, the final outcome was that from the last return filed by John and Mary, an operator keypunched the wrong social security number for Mary and she never existed, according to the i.r.s.

When W-2's and 1099 forms are matched against tax return reporting, Mary's income was never accounted for and the open 1099 income was carried forward and assessed against her in the future when she began filing as a single person.

The only document Mary received was a computer generated letter stating her case had been resolved and no further action was necessary. This poor lady lived almost two years in hell and they did not even say they were sorry!!

A few years ago the i.r.s. was on a rampage to audit taxpayers who were claiming the Earned Income Credit on their return.

The Earned Income Credit is like a subsidy where if your income is less than, let's say, $20,000 and you have two children, you will get an additional refund of about $1,700.

Well, as you can imagine, a whole bunch of taxpayers suddenly had children. (Taxpayers cheat??) Anyway, this caused a wrinkle in someone's jeans at the i.r.s. so a massive investigation was underway.

Several of my clients received notices to verify that they actually had children. Well after a couple of good laughs and a drink or two, these forms still had to be filed. Most taxpayers asked how to answer the form, did it and went on about their business.

Well, one single taxpayer didn't buy this invasion of privacy. (She was not a client of mine). She composed a letter to the i.r.s., relating in gross detail, the birth of both children. To this day they never contacted her again.

While we are on the subject of children, here are a few good quotes relating to parenthood.

~~~~~~~~~~~~~~~~~~~~~~~~~~~~~~~~~~~~

"For adult education, nothing beats children."

"It now costs more to amuse your children than it once did to educate their father."

"Avenge yourself; live long enough to be a problem to your children."

"Be nice to your kids, for it is they who will choose your nursing home."

"There would be fewer problems with children if they had to chop wood to keep the television set going."

"There are three ways to get things done:"
1) Do it yourself
2) Hire someone to do it
3) Forbid your kids to do it

"The best thing to spend on your children is time!"

~~~~~~~~~~~~~~~~~~~~~~~~~~~~~~~~~~~~

Here is a story of i.r.s. agent abuse that really threw me a curve. We will call this "The i.r.s. Stalker Case". Now remember, nothing really surprises me about i.r.s. activities. The dumber the activity the more I seem to understand it. Maybe I have the problem!

Anyway the story goes something like this. Fred and Annabele were informed that their return was selected for additional review by the i.r.s.. They were to bring a number of records to the i.r.s. office and meet with an agent. Their return was really quite simple, so they thought, and gave the whole audit very little consideration.

Fred was a self employed contractor, doing about $300,000 in annual sales. The construction business was on the downside as the economy was suffering from high interest rates. His net profit was not as much as in prior years, so this may have been the red flag signal at the i.r.s.

Fred and Annabele drove up to the i.r.s. building in a car that was about two years old. Annabele dressed very nicely, as she always would when she went out. Fred wore slacks and a shirt.

The items in question were mostly on his business schedule and Fred was not really tuned into financial matters. His forte was to build houses and he left the finances up to his bookkeeper. Well, this did not sit right with the auditor. "Why don't you know this and why don't you know that?", were the standard questions of the auditor.

Nothing was really resolved at the first meeting and Fred asked for more time and would consult with his bookkeeper. The auditor agreed and the meeting ended, so Fred and Annabele thought. Unbeknownst to them, the auditor followed them out and looked at their car. From whatever went through his pea brain, he decided that Fred was a cheater, and there was more to Fred's finances than was showing on the return and other information the i.r.s. thought they had. The case now took on a new look, and life for Fred and Annabele would not be the same for the next few years.

Fred and his bookkeeper met with the auditor another time and proved all of the deductions and transactions that were in question. The audit ended again, so they thought, and nothing more was mentioned.

Several months passed without incident and then one day Annabele noticed the auditor was in her neighborhood grocery store. She didn't think much about it until she saw him again at a shopping mall. (The plot thickens!). She did not want to burden Fred with her observations, but it began to bother her. One night she and Fred went out to dinner and there at the restaurant was the i.r.s. auditor.

Fred and Annabele went home and she told him of the other instances when the auditor was at the same locations as she. This bothered Fred to no end so he called his attorney and related the story. The attorney asked one simple question and that was, "Did you ever receive a clearance from the i.r.s. on the audit results?". "No", Fred related, "What difference does that make?". "My friend, you are still under audit and the i.r.s. agent is checking out your living habits," said the attorney.

The attorney contacted the i.r.s. office and began asking questions about the case and was completely put off by the auditor. A few days later, Fred and his attorney went in person to the i.r.s. office and began asking more questions. This time they got a supervisor and reviewed the case. Although it took time, (about two months), and a lot of patience, they found the files were in order and the audit should have been closed.

As time passed, Fred found out from his associates that the i.r.s. auditor had been asking questions. Annabele heard from neighbors that he also questioned them. No one really wanted to mention anything to Fred and Annabele as they thought it might be an embarrassment to them.

The outcome of this little story is that the auditor took it upon himself to investigate Fred and Annabele. He solely believed Fred was cheating and he was going to make his mark by unveiling a tax fraud case against Fred.

Nothing was ever said about what happened to the auditor. He was probably reprimanded and then sent about his business. This brings us to the next segment of i.r.s. horror stories.

Almost every tax publication I get has stories such as the above and maybe worse. Who gives the i.r.s. the power to invade our privacy and ruin our lives? Story after story relates to instances where the i.r.s. policies of "levies and confiscation procedures" put taxpayers into bankruptcy and stress therapy.

The reason is very simple. There are no checks and balances in the i.r.s.. This was brought out very clearly at recent Senate investigations. The law does not give these people the authority to harass and intimidate. The Ir.'s. procedure manuals do not give these people the authority to harass and intimidate. So why does it happen?

One reason is the Federal Districts have ratings and probably even contests for collecting delinquent tax dollars each quarter or fiscal year. Managers, at all levels, have been found to promote unethical practices to sweeten their career records.

Another reason mentioned on several occasions is when there are no checks and balances, the individual auditors have the option to proceed in any fashion they so desire. This is plain dangerous, as all individuals have a bit of larceny within them. Unrestricted practices produce results and that means money and feathers in someone's cap.

One of the hottest i.r.s. red flag issues is form 1099 income relating to subcontractors. Not only is the i.r.s. hot on this issue, but most of the individual states are too, because they want their fair share of payroll taxes and subcontractors do not pay employment taxes.

A few years back, this issue became so sticky that new guidelines were drawn up by the Treasury that actually gave the employer new life in defending themselves. All i.r.s. agents were to take classes on this subject, but it was not mandatory. Since it was not mandatory, as many as 50% of the agents are not aware of the new laws and guidelines. When they go out and do the audits, they are still acting under the old terms and creating nightmares for the employers.

Employers who can afford to have outside counsel come in and represent them, have done very well against the i.r.s because tax professionals do know the laws, new and old, and seem to love jamming it down the throats of ill mannered and uninformed auditors. I am one of them. I love a good argument.

Will all of this i.r.s. harassment and intimidation ever end? Probably not in the near future. The American public is becoming more knowledgeable, less forgiving, and now is supporting taxpayer advocates more than ever before. We have to change our system of taxation. Flat Tax? Not as we know it today. Modified Flat Tax? Yes. This will be the way to go, but the politicians will always be afraid they might lose something. Sooo, let's get rid of the politicians!!

More horror stories later the book.

If you think some of my opinions are way off the mark, please read on. I'm in good company!

~~~~~~~~~~~~~~~~~~~~~~~~~~~~~~~~~

"This 'telephone' has too many shortcomings to be seriously considered as a means of communication. This device is inherently of no value to us." (Western Union Memo 1876)

"We don't like their sound, and guitar music is on the way out." (Decca Recording Co rejecting the Beatles in 1962)

"Who the hell wants to hear actors talk?" (H.M. Warner, Warner Bros 1927)

~~~~~~~~~~~~~~~~~~~~~~~~~~~~~~~~~

REPORTING INCOME
(We all need more)

Some tax accountant told me that if I put enough technical goodies in this book it might qualify as a tax deductible item for the readers. Worth considering. Hint, Hint !!

Since all taxpayers have a little bit of larceny in them, I want to take this opportunity to tell you readers, DON'T CHEAT ON YOUR TAX RETURN. Now I know this book will qualify as a tax deductible item. The i.r.s. will love me.

I am very serious about not cheating on your taxes. During my 60 years as a tax accountant, I've spent my whole career warning people about the importance of proper reporting of income. It is so darn easy to cheat, or maybe fudge a little, that it becomes a way of life for probably 20% of all taxpayers.

Let's look at some of the reasons why you should not cheat.

The i.r.s. computer system is in complete shambles with an overall rating of 0 to 1. Everyone knows this, (except the i.r.s.), and sooner or later this will be corrected. But, and this is a big but, the i.r.s. has one of the most sophisticated computer programs in the world which gives them the ability to match numbers, people, locations, mother-in-laws, dogs, cats, ex-spouses and everything else.

Because of this, the taxpayer's exact income amounts are sitting there waiting for your tax return to appear. If it does not match, ZAP, they have you cold. Where does this information come from? W-2 and 1099 forms.

Now you certainly didn't think those W-2 and 1099 forms were for your benefit did you? Now they are working on the reverse side of the coin by issuing 1098 and other forms to calculate your deductions. Sneaky little buggers aren't they?

The question I hear quite often now-a-days is how about cash and bartering? Well, the i.r.s. hasn't figured this one out yet, but I'm sure they are working on it. My best advice on these matters is do not tell anyone, least of all your accountant. Your accountant does not have client/accountant privileges, such as doctor/patient or attorney/client, so he is liable for all information you discuss with him should you get into heavy audit cases.

Now that we all agree to report all of our income, we can discuss some of the income items that surprise people at tax time.

State unemployment compensation is fully taxable on the Federal Return. Since there is no tax taken out of this income, it becomes quite a liability at tax time when it increases your taxable income. Very few taxpayers are aware of this. With all of the layoffs we have experience over the years, unemployment compensation has become very common.

State income tax refunds are taxable if you itemize deductions in the prior year. This has been around for years so it is no big surprise?

Inherited property, (stocks, bonds, real estate, etc.), is not considered income in the year received. It will only become taxable when you sell. The cost basis of inherited property is usually the value of the item at the time of death of the donor. When receiving inherited property, have someone find out its value as soon as possible, then keep in your tax files.

Insurance proceeds are generally not taxable, but be sure to check with your tax adviser to verify the taxable status as soon as possible.

Social Security benefits will become taxable at predetermined income levels. This is the number one ripoff towards our senior citizens. Protect yourself with good income planning.

Let's take a time out from all this informative stuff and discuss the taxing of Social Security.

When this tax law passed several years ago, I was livid. I even have to admit the i.r.s. didn't have anything to do with this. Each year I see the Social Security benefits of all my maturing clients. Believe me, they don't get very much.

How some millionaire senator can sit on his fat fanny in Washington, DC and dictate taxing policies on his mother and father's Social Security checks beats the heck out of me. If I was him I would be afraid, (they don't know shame), to go home at Thanksgiving.

Everyday we hear stories and in many cases know of instances where druggies, prostitutes and the such are collecting welfare checks in the amount of $900 to $1200 a month, and it is not taxable. So why are we taxing our elderly? How many Social Security recipients are getting food stamps?

Now let's take a look at the earnings angle of this fiasco. If a Social Security recipient, at age 62-65, earns over $17,000 or so dollars, they will lose Social Security benefits under a complicated formula. If a Social Security recipient is age 65 or over, they can earn as much as they want and not lose benefits.

Come on folks, how many people over age 65 work & earn much money? Our politicians got real generous on this one! How many other civilized countries treat their senior citizens the way our politicians do?

These senior citizens have done their thing. Look at the benefits we Americans have today because of the labor, time and effort put in by our parents and forefathers. Give them a break, you politicians, someday you will be there too!

I feel better now that I got that off my mind! Where were we? Oh yes, income.

Report all interest and dividend income, no matter how small the amounts may be. Remember the 1099 Forms?

Alimony is taxable to the recipient and deductible by the payer, while child support is tax free. Be sure your attorney works hard for you on this one regardless of which side of the fence you are on. More on this in our divorce section.

Early withdrawals, (before age 59 1/2), from IRA/Koegh/SEP retirement accounts become ordinary income and will be taxed in two ways. First it will be included with your other income and taxed accordingly and second it will incur a 10% penalty that will be added to your tax liability. Another big surprise at tax time.

Best Bet: Always rollover your retirement accounts by having the old fund send a check to your new fund. Please do not have the check made out to you! There are at least three tax traps on rollovers. Consult a tax adviser before each transaction.

Let's spend a little time talking about 1099 forms of income. There are 1099's for interest, dividends, rents and royalties. The one that concerns me and causes most of the problems is the 1099 forms sent to you as a non- employee or subcontractor.

This has become one of the most important targets in audit proceedings and is very serious business. I can only touch on the subject and bring it to your attention.

There are three main tax traps with 1099 reporting. All of the following have actually happened to a client or someone who came to me for consultation. Unfortunately, these examples have occurred many, many times.

1) Employer/payer say they will pay you under the table so there will not be any deductions and you   will take home more money. The truth is, they do not want to file payroll tax returns and have to pay some 12% in payroll taxes plus another 3-8% in worker's compensation insurance. But here is the catch in many cases. At year end the payer's accountant tells them that they cannot legally deduct your pay unless there is a 1099 form filed, (this is required by law with stiff penalties). So you receive a 1099 form listing all that money as income with no deductions for income taxes. WOW, do you ever have a tax problem!

2) Employer/payer cheats on their income taxes. One area available to them is to overstate 1099 pay to non-employees. Now, unless you have been keeping good track of your pay, (and most people don't), their 1099 form amount will go on your tax return and you will never know the difference.

3) Bad timing: Employer/payer writes a check to you on December 31 for work done that month, but you do not receive the check until January 10thor later. That check will be income to you in the prior year, although you did not receive it until some time in the middle of January. What do you do? If the the check is for a small amount, I would pay the taxes on it and let the matter go. If the check is for a large amount I would take exception to the the 1099 form on your tax return and report the proper amount. Then include the January check in next year's tax return.

More on 1099, (non-employee pay), forms and the problems that they can cause will be discussed in the business section. There, we will discuss the employers' side of the problems.

> Caution: 1099 income for non-employee compensation is subject to Social Security Taxes.

DEDUCTIONS FROM INCOME
(Notice how small this section is?)

Always put as much as possible into a retirement plan whether it be at work or into an IRA on your own. This is your best investment for asset accumulation over the years. I believe it now tops owning your home as the number one investment for the average American.

New tax legislation, starting in 1998, had a few new IRA accounts available to the average worker. Some of the penalties are being liberalized on early withdrawals, (before age 59 1/2). See your tax adviser!

Moving expenses are deductible, (again), without having to itemize. This is a real tax break for renters who normally can not itemize deductions. There are several restrictions so be careful when you use this deduction! And remember to save all of your moving receipts.

Alimony paid is deducted in this section. Be sure to list your ex spouses social security number and address.

Self-employed individuals may deduct 100% of their health insurance premiums in this section of the return. For those taxpayers who itemize, you may deduct the balance of health insurance premiums with your other medical bills.

School teachers may deduct $250 of school supplies paid out of pocket. The balance of these items can be deducted if you itemize deduction.

Student loan interest is deducted in this section.
Tuition and fees are deducted in this section.

As you can see, the politicians made this a very short section of the tax return.

~~~~~~~~~~~~~~~~~~~~~~~~~~~~~~~~~~~~~~~

A POINT TO MEASURE

If you need to measure something in a hurry and there is no ruler available, try this! Take a piece of currency out of your wallet, (if you are like me it will only be a dollar), and lay it out. This will give you 6". Fold it in half and you will have 3". Fold the half in half and you will have 1½" Now, if you are really in the chips, you can use two one dollar bills and measure 12". Whoopie!!

~~~~~~~~~~~~~~~~~~~~~~~~~~~~~~~~~~~~~~~

I

TEMIZED DEDUCTIONS
(Be sure you have good records)

Since this book is not intended to be a guideline or text, we will only be reviewing certain areas that most taxpayers don't really understand, or are not familiar with.

MEDICAL DEDUCTIONS
Medical deductions are getting harder to use each year since the heavy emphasis on health insurance and HMO's in recent years. One deduction that is commonly overlooked is mileage to and from medical appointments.

TAXES
In the taxes section, remember to include property taxes on boats, motorhomes and other licensed toys. In the "other taxes" section you can deduct a part of your automobile license fee and state disability insurance deducted from your paycheck.

INTEREST
Under the interest deduction you will see a section for deducting points paid. When a lender reports points on a 1098 form, you will list that amount with your other mortgage interest. When you refinance your principal residence or take out a loan on a second home, there are different rules for reporting points paid.

Points paid on refinancing, etc. must be deducted over the period of your loan, (15-20-30 years).

This makes the deduction very small and sometimes overlooked. Where you have to be careful is when you sell the property. You can deduct the remaining balance of the points in the year of sale. I would guess this deduction is overlooked 50% of the time.

Interest paid to credit card companies and other personal interest is no longer deductible. One exception to the rule is when you incur credit card interest on business related transactions. This portion may be deducted as a business expense.

CHARITABLE CONTRIBUTIONS

When giving to charity, whether in property or cash, always get a receipt. We all give money to someone on the street and no receipt is available and that's all right. But any other time, a receipt is almost a must.

Volunteer workers may deduct expenses related to working charitable events. The most overlooked deduction is auto expenses. You may claim a standard mileage rate for miles driven or deduct the actual costs, whichever is greater.

There are big tax breaks when giving large amounts of money or property, especially with appreciated property. Always consult with a tax adviser, before you do anything, to get the maximum tax benefit.

CASUALTY LOSSES

Most taxpayers don't understand this section of the tax return and neither do a whole lot of tax preparers. It becomes a very technical tax deduction and should not be discussed here. Just remember that if you have an auto accident, robbery or property damage be sure to mention this to your tax adviser as there could be a good deduction available to you.

OTHER DEDUCTIONS

This is the "catch all" section of your tax return. A good tax accountant can fill this area with all kinds of good deductions if you sit down and talk to them. This is when you really need to keep all of your receipts, (which very few people do now-a-days).

Under this section, you may be able to deduct employee expenses, job hunting expenses, home office expenses, investment expenses, continuing education, computer, teacher's school supplies, uniforms, tools, employee auto expenses, job related expenses, professional dues and many more.

Many taxpayers get confused when we talk about the standard deduction and the itemized deductions. The i.r.s. allows a set deduction each year of around $6,000 for single persons and about $12,000 for married couples. You have these amounts automatically available on your tax return.

If taxpayers are purchasing a home, they will have mortgage interest and this deduction alone will normally be $5,000 to $10,000 a year, so they can itemize their deduction along with the other items we discussed above.

Without the large amount of interest and maybe some heavy medical bills, it is almost impossible to itemize your deductions.

O.K. readers, school is out. No more technical tax return goodies from here on. If you haven't learned how to reduce you taxes by now, then you never will.

~~~~~~

Here is an unlikely story, but kind of cute:

The taxman was surprised to receive a letter which read, "Dear Sir, Last year I cheated on my tax return   and I can't sleep for thinking about it. I am there-fore enclosing a check for $2,000 dollars. If I find that I still can't sleep, I'll send you the balance."

~~~~~~

Another one? Here is a quote by a good old American:

~~~~~~

"I'm proud to be paying taxes in the United States.
The only thing is, I could be just as proud for half the money."
(Arthur Godfrey)

~~~~~~~~~~~~~~~~~~~~~~~~~~~~~~~

We still have room on this page so let's put in another i.r.s. story:

~~~~~~~~~~~~~~~~~~~~~~~~~~~~~~~

One mosquito to another "Sure I believe in reincarnation –
in my previous life I was an i.r.s. agent!" - -

 Bob Thaves (Frank & Ernest)

~~~~~~~~~~~~~~~~~~~~~~~~~~~~~~~~

A GOOD TAX ADVISER
(How to find one?)

What is a good tax adviser and how do you find one? This question haunts many taxpayers. Someone who only has wages and a little bit of interest, etc. can probably go to any tax service. Almost any tax preparer can complete a simple return and and will charge a reasonable fee.

When you own a home, have a business or a variety of investments, choosing a tax preparer becomes more difficult and I believe a very important part of your financial affairs.

I started doing income taxes in 1956. From 1956 through 1975, the tax laws changed, but not as radically as they have from that date on. The first big change I experienced was in 1976 when they completely changed the tax return. This was one of their first attempts at tax simplification. Their thinking, I believe, was to add line after line of information so the taxpayer could easily identify income and deduction items.

Well folks, they were wrong, as usual, and 1976 tax filing was one of the biggest tax fiascoes in history. There were so many tax preparation errors, by individuals and professionals, that nothing was right.

The form was easy enough to follow, but the i.r.s. had different views of what was to go on each line than the average tax professional. I made some mistakes and when they came to light, I was amazed at the i.r.s. interpretation of the tax form. I spoke with several tax associates and they were having the same problems and were completely confused.

From 1976 to the present day, the federal government has changed the tax laws, the tax forms, the tax philosophy and everything else you can think of, almost every year. If they missed a year, they sure made up for it the following time around.

In 1986, they made some real serious changes in our tax laws. They completely eliminated tax shelters and almost all tax benefits. They were out for the almighty dollar and they were not going to lose any revenues through the income tax filing system.

From 1986 through 1996 they did their thing each year, but were not really satisfied with the results. Things were going too smoothly. So in 1997, they came up with the "1997 Taxpayer Relief Act" This is a beauty. They reduced the capital gains tax. They gave special credits for children, college, selling a home and approved some new IRA accounts. So far so good, right? Well folks, this was all done in such haste that the laws were never finalized. Now the taxpayer is at the mercy of the i.r.s. for interpretation of the new laws. This is really scary. DON'T EVER LET THE I.R.S. INTERPRET ANYTHING!!

Due to the last 20 years of tax law and tax form changes, it is becoming very difficult to choose the right tax preparer. Every phase of the income tax law has now become a specialty. Unfortunately, you can not go to one tax adviser for a portion of your return and to another for another portion. It has to be prepared and signed by only one individual or firm.

Over the past few years, I have turned down the opportunity to prepare tax returns due to their complexity. I decided many years ago that I was going to specialize in returns of the average taxpayer and those with small businesses.

I used to do corporation, partnership, estate and trust returns and never worried about what I didn't know. Then when the tax laws started changing every year, I sat back and gave the situation a lot of thought. The tax world was changing and I had better change with it.

I knew the small business world backwards and forwards as I owned about 20 or so small businesses over the years. I knew the investment world in a like manner as I invested in just about everything. But as the tax laws became more and more complicated, I found that I was unable to answer the questions as quickly and completely as I once did and that put the big question mark in my mind.

I am very happy doing individual returns and working with small businesses. I am a highly regarded expert and have a wonderful reputation. My question is how many other tax preparers have taken note as to where they stand and what they are doing?

There is no right way to choose your tax adviser. I will list some do's and don'ts and hopefully this will shed some light on your individual situation.

1) Never go to a tax preparer who charges a fee based on the amount of your refund. This is illegal and very unethical.

2) Never go to a tax preparer who claims that his clients never get audited. Audits are part of the tax world and they will always exist.

3) Never go to a tax preparer who offers tax advice along the lines of under reporting income or fudging expenditures. This is a very common practice among inexperienced tax people. They want to impress you. They believe that getting clients refunds will build their business. This is also illegal and very unethical.

4) Watch out for the tax preparer who knows it all. The better the tax preparer, the less they know. Believe me!

5) A good tax preparer will not give legal advice. I had five years of law in school and forty plus years of experience. I am aware of most legal consequences. I never give legal advice. I do tell my clients that there may be legal implications involved and advise them to speak with an attorney.

6) A good tax preparer will spend time interviewing the clients. No matter how long I have worked with a client, I still spend time asking questions. Remember, people and the times are always changing. Some of the commercial tax firms can not afford the time

to properly interview clients and they do miss some very pertinent information.

7) The larger the tax firm, the less time you will receive. Just as in any business, time is money and the tax world is no different. Large tax firms have time quotas that are strictly enforced. Besides you do not need a large tax firm to prepare most taxpayers' returns.

8) The best way to find a good tax person is to ask a friend. If they are happy with the work and feel comfortable when talking to this person, then you may have a winner.

9) It is very important for you to like and trust your tax preparer. For some reason, people do not want to discuss their finances. Most people just plain dislike numbers and taxes are all about numbers. This in turn makes people dislike taxes, regardless of why we have taxes. I have found that people hate numbers more than the i.r.s. and that is making quite a statement. This also makes it very hard to extract information from clients.

10) If you are happy with your tax person, do not change. Finding a new one may be very difficult. If you do not feel comfortable with your tax person, then make a change right away. There is no reason to add fuel to an already bad situation. And tax time is always a bad situation. (I can't believe I said that!)

DO YOU FEEL LIKE THIS
WITH YOUR TAX PREPARER?

When you are talking with a new tax preparer, there are certain questions that you should ask. Since it is your money they are working with, be sure they are qualified. Here are some good questions to ask:

1) Ask about their educational background. What makes them a qualified tax return preparer?

2) How long have they been doing taxes and where did they get their experience?

3) What are the fees for preparing your tax return? Don't ever accept the answer that they don't know. I know exactly what the return will cost the client and I give them a fee amount. Sometimes there will be additional schedules that may be required like depreciation or business expenses. If they have a lot of equipment or expenses I will give a close estimate.

4) How long will it take to do your return? When can I expect to pick it up? Don't give them an option to put your return aside while they work on others.

5) Last, but not least, ask them if they will represent you before the i.r.s. should there be a problem. This is a very important question because a good taxperson is not afraid of the i.r.s. I would guess that 80% or more of the tax preparers will not represent you before the i.r.s. They are so unqualified and so unsure of themselves that the audit will become a nightmare, more to them than you, and you are the taxpayer!

There are several different types of tax preparers in the marketplace. We should discuss them so you will be aware of who you are talking to.

The best way to list the types of tax preparers is according to their specialties. This does not mean they are better or worse than the others, as some of my stories in this book will illustrate.

1) C.P.A.'s are noted as tax specialist. They are licensed by the state and in most cases very thorough and detail minded. They probably charge the most.

2) Attorneys, (my favorite people), are very qualified individuals. They normally do not specialize in taxes, but there are many C.P.A./Tax attorneys and they are sharp. These people will charge an arm and a leg.

3) Enrolled Agents are individuals who have had special schooling and passed a very difficult test. They are licensed to practice before the i.r.s. This title makes up an elite group of tax professionals.

4) Registered Tax Return Preparer. A new classification where they too are required to have continuing education each year and take a test.

The four groups listed above are generally very qualified and are required to take continuing education courses each year to maintain their licensed status.

4) Accountants and bookkeepers file a lot of tax returns each year. Most of them do not have additional tax education, but they will have knowledge of filing tax returns.

5) Former and current i.r.s. employees. These people think they know it all. Very few of them know anything, let alone how to file a proper tax return. These people get tax clients to believe that since they are, or were i.r.s. personnel they know all of the tricks. Well folks I have to disagree. There are some very qualified personnel at the i.r.s. We will discuss them in the section on audits. Most of the tax returns I have seen prepared by i.r.s. people, that have any kind of advance tax computations, are not prepared very professionally.

6) Everyone wants to get into the tax prep business during the first four months of the year. There is good money in preparing taxes. Here is where we see a complete breakdown in tax return preparation. Now that we have computers and probably 100 tax programs on the market, we also have the new generation of tax

experts. Now, believe me when I say that to file a tax return is really easy if you do not know what you are doing. There were so many new tax return preparers in 1994 through 1996 that I'm surprised to still be in business. For $10 you can have your return completed. I would recommend that you plan to pay a little more than that! No need to say anything else.

The problem of finding a good tax preparer will always be with us. Take the time to research the person you are going to trust with your tax money. In the future the tax preparation fees will be increasing. This is due to the new tax laws and the complexity of future tax returns.

It has become very apparent that when the government gives you some tax break, or takes one away, they will always bury their move with a more complicated tax return. They have done this with the medical and dental fields. They do it all the time with legal entanglement and now it is time to do it in a big way with the accounting and tax field.

This would be a good time to insert a couple of sayings. One is very well known, while the other is less publicized, but very fitting.

We have all heard and seen this one. I personally live my life accordingly.

"TODAY IS THE FIRST DAY
OF THE REST OF YOUR LIFE"

The following statement is a favorite of mine and has so many implications that it can be applied to almost any phase of life.

"YOU WILL KEEP ON GETTING
WHAT YOU HAVE BEEN GETTING
IF YOU KEEP ON DOING
WHAT YOU HAVE BEEN DOING"

What these sayings have to do with taxes is way beyond me, but I just wanted to give you some food for thought.

I CAN'T PAY MY TAX BILL
(Shame on You)

The biggest surprise at tax time is when the client finds out they are not getting back a refund. It seems to be happening more and more now, since there are so many two income earners in each family.

Most taxpayers don't give taxes any thought during the year. Should the taxpayer's situation change, such as getting a nice raise or in many cases getting married or divorced, their tax return completely changes.

With any change, the tax bill will always get bigger and the good old days of refunds are long gone. How can we avoid this problem? That's easy. Don't get married, divorced or accept a raise.

My standard answer to the situation is keep your tax adviser informed of any changes that occur during the year. A simple phone call can save you a lot of headaches and tax dollars. Most people are afraid that they will be charged when you ask a tax person a question. Although this may be true in some cases, I have found that many tax preparers can give you a simple solution in a matter of minutes, and there will be no charge.

The following is a list of some of the standard questions I receive during the year and how I would answer them without charging.

1) I recently married and my new spouse works and earns XX dollars, should we make any changes? Without giving this much thought I could answer: For the remainder of the year, leave your exemptions as they are. You will have more than adequate withholding taken at the single rate. If the take home pay amount is a problem, then we would need to sit down and recalculate taxes to your current situation. A nice refund would be a wonderful wedding present.

2) I recently got divorced, what do I do? A simple answer would be to change your withholding to single with no dependents. This half of the coin becomes more complicated than getting married, due to the many options available to divorced couples. We will deal with this in our divorce section.

3) We bought a house. Won't this help eliminate our tax bill? The answer to this is: When was the house purchased and how many mortgage payments will be made in the current tax year? If the purchase was made early in the year, it will benefit taxpayers. If the purchase was made during the summer or fall, there will be very little tax benefits for the current year. Why? There will be only a few mortgage payments made and the interest will be minimal.

4) We purchased some rental property, won't this lower our taxes? This answer will be similar to the house question above except tax payers can benefit from depreciation. Again, the question regarding the date of purchase is the determining factor. Rental depreciation is sometimes very small.

Those are the four basic questions I receive during the year. The biggest change in a taxpayers situation comes from earning more money. Taxpayers who were receiving the "Earned Income Credit", based on a lower income, are the ones who are surprised the most. Each year they would be getting a big refund due to the extra money refunded from the "Earned Income Credit". When their income increases and they don't qualify anymore, zap! No refund, and in many cases they now have a tax bill.

What do you do if you owe a tax bill and are unable to pay on April 15th? Yell and scream at your tax preparer! It has to be their fault, right? Unfortunately I have been yelled at several times. I didn't know I had so many names as I hear at this particular time. They don't know this. but I feel worse about the situation than they do, as I'm the one who has to tell them. Have you ever fired an employee? Same kind of feeling. These things can really tear at your stomach.

There are several options available when taxes are due. The following responses have been simplified to make the situation more understandable.

1) Always file the tax return when due!

2) Always send some money along with the return. Something is better then nothing.

3) If the return is not paid in full, you will receive a nasty letter from the i.r.s. To show you their appreciation, they will give you a penalty and some interest to pay. I love these guys!!

4) If the balance is small, pay what you can and send them a check on your next payday. Just remember to file that return on time. Do Not hold back filing the return because of a short payment. They will really give you a tax penalty for not filing on time.

5) The above cases are really simplified and probably happen millions of times a year. When the tax bill gets to an outrageous amount, another whole approach needs to be addressed. We have to work on having the i.r.s. accept payments on account. They are very good about doing this, only they will add the penalties and interest, and before you know it you have one big monster on your back. They will make your car payment and mortgage look like pocket change. Your tax adviser can give you details on this process.

Where do all these large tax bills come from? If you have wages and withholding, this problem is something like we mentioned above. The real problem comes from self employed persons and those with big capital gains and large income producing assets.

Self employed persons and investors are supposed to file estimated taxes each quarter of the year. This is like withholding from your paycheck. A kind of pay as you go philosophy. Because there is no way for the government to collect money from these individuals during the year, they kind of put you on the honor system. (I keep telling you these i.r.s. folks are not very smart).

Most of these types of taxpayers are very honest and pay their quarterly estimates. But, we have a whole group of taxpayers out there that look at not paying quarterly taxes during the year as a little financial bonus to them. They think the i.r.s. doesn't need the money as much as they do. Wrong!

Self employed persons are probably the worst offenders when it comes to not paying quarterly income taxes. The reason being that cash flow is never enough to cover the monthly expenses. The only creditor they are not in daily contact with is the i.r.s., so they pay them last if anything is left over.

One of the most important rules of business is do not use tax money to pay other bills. This applies to payroll tax money as well as income tax money.

I have several clients who do not pay estimated taxes. For up to 20 years I have preached the tax gospel to them and they still will not pay estimated taxes. I am not a policemen, nor am I their daily reminder service. These taxpayers pay $3,000 to $10,000 in tax penalties and interest every year and they think that is cheap money. What do I know?

Most taxpayers are working at a regular job with taxes being withheld. As mentioned before this will normally cover your taxes for the year. One thing that is overlooked is the investment side of your financial picture. If you have substantial investments, it is almost certain that you will need to make quarterly estimates along with your regular withholding.

What many taxpayers do to avoid making quarterly estimates is have an extra amount withheld from their paycheck. This is just as effective and you don't have to worry about filing on a quarterly basis.

There are a lot of tricks to paying quarterly taxes. If you are making money outside of normal wages, talk to your tax adviser and see if he can give you some pointers along these lines. There are options available to your situation.

How about a couple of quotes to keep you awake?

~~~~~~~~~~~~~~~~~~~~~~~~~~~~~~~

"Ninety percent of the politicians give
the other ten percent a bad name"
(Henry Kissinger)

~~~~~~~~~~~~~~~~~~~~~~~~~~~~~~~

"Tell a man there are 300 billion stars in
the universe and he'll believe you. Tell
him a bench has wet paint on it and he'll
have to touch it to be sure."
(Jarger)

~~~~~~~~~~~~~~~~~~~~~~~~~~~~~~~

DIVORCE AND SEPARATION
(A very difficult time in life)

This is the most difficult area to deal with when it comes to income taxes. The tax portion I can handle, but when you are interviewing clients, emotions run deep and I see a lot of pain.

I have been there and so have many of you readers. I would have liked to skip over this chapter, but the importance of the tax implications are too great to leave out of this book.

When reading this chapter, please don't think that any of my writings are indicating legal advice. I do not give legal advice as I am certainly not qualified. I will be discussing many areas that get pretty sticky and you may conclude that I am giving the gospel on divorce proceedings and tax consequences. I am only trying to bring certain pertinent facts to the table to inform readers in areas I believe should be addressed.

Federal Income tax laws apply to all of our 50 states. There is no difference between taxpayers in New York and those in California. On many occasions there have been different rulings in tax courts from one district to another. Why? I haven't the slightest idea. Federal Law should be Federal Law, without exception.

When it comes to divorce, state laws dictate the proceedings and the federal laws are secondary, if at all considered. This makes applying income tax philosophy very difficult in divorces.

One simple way to relate to the income tax problems caused by divorce is the fact that the i.r.s. is not a party to the divorce proceedings. No matter what you and your spouse may have agreed upon and entered into your divorce decree, the i.r.s. may collect taxes from either party on a prior joint return.

Let's use an example in one of our i.r.s. horror stories. Now is as good a time as any to start telling our stories again.

Sam and Sally were married for 20 years when they decided to call it quits. They had filed joint income tax returns every year and never had any problems. Sam was a self employed painting contractor and built up a very successful business. Sally did the bookkeeping for the business during the first 12 years. As the kids entered school, she thought it best for her to stay at home, so she would be there whenever they needed her.

Their divorce was not a happy one, but the two parties agreed on almost everything. Sally was to receive the house, had custody of the two children, and received a comfortable monthly income. The attorneys had worked out a reasonable split between alimony and child support.

Sally and Sam had decided to file a joint return for their last year in marriage, even though they did not live together for the full year. The separation and divorce proceedings started in one year and ended in the next. Sam and his accountant filed the tax returns and as far as Sally was concerned everything seemed to be on the up and up. One of the settlements in the proceedings was that Sam was to pay the balance of taxes due on their last joint return.

Sam began to have business problems and fell behind in his payments to Sally. Not only was he short on Sally's payments, but with the rest of his creditors as well. Sally thought this to be very irregular, as Sam was a stickler for paying his bills. When she confronted him, he became evasive and Sally started to see another side of the man she was married to for over 20 years.

Sally saw the handwriting on the wall and decided she had better get a job to supplement her alimony. Her parents had left her some inheritance, so there was money in the kitty, but how long would it last? When the alimony and child support payments stopped, Sally was in pretty good shape and was able to meet her and the children's daily needs.

Two years had passed when Sally received a letter from the i.r.s. stating that there was a balance due on the joint income tax return filed during their last year of marriage. Sam had closed down his painting business and was living with, and sponging off, his new girlfriend. He started to hit the booze in a big way.

Sally went to her attorney and asked all the proper questions. The attorney filed papers to get Sam back into court, but to no avail. Sam was getting good at the dodge and duck game used by so many deadbeats of his kind. Her attorney's contention was that Sam was the responsible party for the back taxes, as it was so stated in the divorce papers.

As time passed, the i.r.s. was getting impatient and sending notices to Sally on a regular basis. Interest and penalties were piling up and the original tax bill had almost doubled. Now it was time for the good old property seizure notices to appear and sure enough Sally's wages were attached and so was her bank account.

Sally, fighting to support her two children, had to contend with the i.r.s. who was attaching everything they could to satisfy their quotas without ever considering the consequences it placed on Sally and her family.

Sally got hold of her tax adviser who worked out a repayment schedule with the i.r.s.. Sally had to get this tax lien off her back or she would never be able to get credit again and continue to support her two children through the very difficult years of high school and college.

What does this little horror story tell us? Sally let the first few notices slip by her as she was convinced that Sam was responsible for the income taxes. Why? The divorce decree said it was to be. Wrong! Next we can conclude that Sally's attorney was not paying attention when it came to income taxes, as there should have been some kind of checks and balances in the negotiations, as to paying off the remaining bills of the marriage. Last, but not least, the i.r.s. doesn't care about any settlements worked out in the course of divorce proceedings. They are not a party to the contract and all they want is their money. Where it comes from and how they get it is of no concern to them. Both parties are liable for income taxes filed by joint return.

Please remember that when negotiating who pays what and when, there has to be assurances that you will know they have been paid. Especially income taxes!

Let's spend a little bit of time talking about attorneys. As you know, these are some of my favorite people. Case after case of divorce stories I read have chilling stories about how the attorneys miss the boat in negotiating settlements. There are a lot of good attorneys in the world. They are sharp and pay attention to their work. Then we seem to have the attorneys that go outside of their specialty field and this is where I see most of the problems.

When you are having marital problems and a divorce seems like the only way out, see an attorney that specializes in divorces. Too many people go to the family attorney or a friend who may specialize in civil proceedings. These people don't know the "ins and outs" of divorces. They take the cases as a gesture of friendship, or better yet, greed. I have never seen an attorney turn down money!

What is the difference between being separated and getting a divorce when it comes to income taxes?

Let's start out with a separated couple. There are so many things to consider that there is no right or wrong way to file income taxes. This is when the situation, and the people involved, will dictate the proper way to file the tax return.

1) No children in the marriage.
When you are separated and there has been no final decree issued, nor a legal separation granted, the couple can file "Jointly" or as "Married person filing a separate return". Filing a joint return will, in most cases, save you tax dollars. Due to circumstances and attitudes of the people involved, this may not be a wise thing to do. If this is the case, then you would have to file as a "Married person filing a separate return".

If there has been a legal separation, while the divorce is being finalized, then each spouse must file as "Single". Legally separated persons can not file a joint return.

2) There are children in the marriage.
When there are children of the marriage, we have additional considerations to filing tax returns. The above rules apply, only we have one extra filing status to use that can be very beneficial. This is called "Head of Household". "Head of Household" tax rates are higher then "Joint" filing rates, but lower than "Single" or "Married filing separate return".

As usual with the i.r.s., there are limitations to taking this deduction and several test items have to be met.

To simplify matters, I will skip all of the legal stuff and list the main substance. If you are legally separated or divorced, and have custody of the children, you may claim "Head of Household" as long as you are the main support person, (paying over 50% of their expenses). If you are only paying 50% or less of their expenses, then you will need to have a special form signed by the other parent. See your tax adviser.

If you and your spouse are not legally separated, then we have one more item to consider. If you and your spouse did not live together for the last six months of the year, then the parent with custody of the children may claim "Head of Household" and receive the lower tax benefits.

In all cases, the custodial parent has to provide the main home for the children for more then six months of the year. If there is joint custody and the children alternate between the mother and father and neither parent has custody for over six months, then no parent may claim the children as a deduction or receive "Head of Household" status. This again is where the special form has to be filed. See your tax adviser.

If the previous paragraphs seem vague, your assumption is correct. There is no way that I could list all of the circumstances involved in divorces and separations. I am only trying to bring things to your attention. The above represents the main items involved in filing a tax return for separated couples.

When couples are legally divorced, their filing status automatically changes to "Single". The only exception to this rule is when there are children involved. The "Head of Household" rules apply that we discussed earlier.

~~~~~~~~~~~~~~~~~~~~~~~~~~~~~

"Never go to bed mad, stay up and fight"
(Phyllis Diller)

~~~~~~~~~~~~~~~~~~~~~~~~~~~~~

Here is an unusual question along the lines of married, divorced and separated. "I was married for a little over one year. The marriage was annulled during the second year. During the first year we filed a joint tax return. What do I do?"

Because a decree of annulment means that no valid marriage ever existed, you are considered unmarried for both years in the eyes of the i.r.s.. You will need to file an amended return for the year you filed jointly and claim the "Single" status, unless there are children involved and then you can use "Head of Household"

When a marriage begins to break down, the people involved seem to be the last ones to find out about it. How many people going through divorces have had friends tell them all of the things they had noticed, long before you, that the marriage was falling apart? Why don't they tell you as they see it and maybe a lot of divorces could be avoided?

What questions do you ask your attorney? I'm sure the most standard question is, "How did this happen?" My list of questions will only be tax related, but you will see how much of the divorce we cover.

I have always been amazed at how little emphasis is put on income taxes in a divorce. Some attorneys really overlook the importance of income taxes, but as you will see, tax implications go very, very deep.

The most common procedure in a divorce is a good property settlement. Division of marital property, with exceptions, is not taxable to either party. If you plan to sell assets before the divorce and split the proceeds, then you are asking for tax problems. Tax will be due on any profit made on the asset sale. Best bet is to work out an equitable split that will be tax free.

Alimony and child support will probably be second on the list. Here is where you really need your attorney to work hard for you. Alimony is taxable to the recipient and deductible by the payer. Child support is non-taxable and non-deductible by the parties. Shrewd attorneys can really play around with this area. One attorney will go big for alimony and minimize the child support, while another may do the reverse, contending that the total dollars end up the same. When you consider tax implications and future earnings, you will find out that the total dollar philosophy may not be in your best interest. Always demand a fair split and do some calculating.

Along with the child support/alimony question comes the dependent deduction. Who gets to claim the children and so on. Many hurt parties to a divorce are in such a hurry to get rid of the other spouse that they agree to anything. Please think this through very carefully.

The new "Taxpayers Relief Act of 1997" will cause some new child support questions and problems. Within the tax act there is a provision for getting a credit for paying college tuition and an additional credit for each child claimed as a dependent. The person who is allowed the dependent exemption will be the one allowed the above credits. If one person pays the bills and another claims the dependent exemptions, then no one can get the credits. This is going to be a big area for negotiations. Again, please pay attention!

Next in line might be the 401K plan or IRA accounts. Over the years, these funds have become very large and each spouse is entitled to their fair share earned during the marriage. As a side note, the division of a retirement account and the withdrawal of funds before age 59 1/2, due to divorce, is not taxable nor penalized by the i.r.s. if the split balances are rolled over to a new IRA account.

~~~~~~~~~~~~~~~~~~~~~~~~~~~~~~~~~~~~~~

"You should never criticize your spouse's judgement -- look who they decided to marry!!!

"Marriage is nature's way of keeping people from fighting with strangers."
(Someone anonymus)

~~~~~~~~~~~~~~~~~~~~~~~~~~~~~~~~~~~~~~

The most common type of property in a marriage is the family home. In some instances there will be a vacation home and some business property. How to divide up interests in these properties has always been a problem.

When there is not enough cash or other equities in the marriage to offset property values, the attorneys really have to earn their fees. There are many ways to negotiate settlements, but the parties have to use some creative thinking and planning.

 I am a firm believer that the property that benefits one party more than the other should retain title and use. An example of this would be: The main residence should go to the person who has custody of the children. Any business property should go to the person who is best at conducting the business, etc.. By doing this, each party is getting the best value and you are not in any way inhibiting the other party from producing income. Too many parties want to hurt the other and they do not consider the consequences down the road.

Never, and I repeat, never, keep the other party from producing income that will be paying the alimony, child support and future expenses. I have seen so many cases where the parties in a divorce self- destruct and after they get past their hurt feelings and emotional distress find themselves in a sorry financial condition.

The best way to divide up property, whether there is only one asset or a full portfolio, is to buy each other out. You know the old saying, "One marble for you and one for me". If one of the marbles is bigger, then negotiate the difference in value and continue separating the marbles.

Let me tell you a story about Larry and Liz. This is not one of my i.r.s. horror stories. The i.r.s. had nothing to do with this situation, but as always, they will eventually stick their nose into our story before we're finished.

Larry was a computer programmer and Liz was a successful interior designer. Larry found that a program he was developing could be expanded and with some creative marketing and financing, open up a whole new world in the travel business.

Larry found some financial backers and opened up a small company to market the new program. He enjoyed instant success and with many other new products right behind it, Larry and his friends were on their way to becoming computer millionaires.

Liz quit her job and they began having the family they always wanted. Within three years, their little family grew to four children. (Yes, they had twins!) With their success came the purchase of the vacation home, rental property and a nice stock portfolio. Larry bought a warehouse that was converted to meet the needs of his business, then he rented it back to his corporation. Larry and Liz were at the apex of their careers.

Twelve years had passed before any problems began to appear. The business was pulling Larry in one direction and the household responsibilities were pulling Liz in another. Their perfect little world was beginning to crumble. Larry was coming home every night, but it seemed to be getting later and later. His business trips became more frequent and lasted longer.

Finally, one night the two of them sat down and had the long talk they both knew was coming. They had grown apart over the years and and the love between them became more like respect and the bonding had been broken. Larry did not have any special "other" person in mind nor did Liz. Their problem was the change in lifestyle and responsibilities led them down different paths of life and interests.

Since they were still very good friends and no financial problems were between them they decided to use the family lawyer for the divorce.

A very generous division of property was made to both parties. Whatever benefited Larry and his business was his and Liz was rewarded with other assets to make the division equitable. Larry's business interests were widespread and consisted of a vast amount of real estate. Some of the real estate was purchased by the family, as individuals, and leased back to the corporations while others were bought by the corporations outright. The purchases were made according to good tax planning that would benefit the family as a whole.

Because the family was splitting up, arrangements had to be made to get the real estate back in the hands of Larry and his corporations. To help fatten Liz's kitty, the attorney allocated the family owned corporate properties to Liz and she would in turn sell them back to the corporations for a tidy profit. Installment sale arrangements were made so the income would flow to Liz over a long period of time, thus supplementing her alimony.

Liz was awarded the custody of the children and the family residence. Larry was to pay a large amount of child support and a minimum amount of alimony due to the fact that Liz had stocks, bonds and the business real estate that was going to be sold back to the corporations. The attorney thought he did a marvelous job, charged them an arm and a leg, drew up all the papers and wished them both the best.

Well, you know we can't have the story end here. It just isn't in the cards and we don't have any income tax implications anywhere.

Liz and the kids had to do some adjusting without Larry and, although it was very hard on them, time seemed to heal all wounds. They were very comfortable as Larry had provided them well. The alimony and child support checks came like clockwork and mortgages from the real estate sales were always paid on time.

About three years after the divorce, the child support payments dropped by 25%. The oldest child had reached the age of 18 and the support payment stopped. The next year the twins were 18 and again the child support payments dropped by 67%. This was beginning to bother Liz as the money wasn't coming in, yet the expenses were still there and she had college tuition's, etc. to contend with.

Liz phoned the old family attorney and started to complain. "Ah, come on Liz, you knew this was going to happen, etc and so on," was his response. Liz was livid, but she never really read the divorce papers and did not ever consider there would be a drop in income. She still had plenty of money to draw from so the matter was soon forgotten.

The fourth year after the divorce Liz got a notice from the i.r.s. stating that they had questions regarding her reporting of interest that did not match up to the 1099 interest forms. The corporation was claiming they paid Liz a certain amount of Interest on the purchase of the real estate, but it did not match up to her return. The i.r.s. also contended that there was a profit made on the sale of the real estate and that also did not appear on her tax returns.

An audit was performed and sure enough Liz and her tax accountant did not include interest paid by the corporation as income, nor did they include the profit on the sales. They both contended that it was part of the divorce's division of property, which is not taxable.

The tax accountant wanted Liz to take this to tax court. He would represent her and he felt she had a very good case and was going to win. All of a sudden she found herself in a real mess. Her income was reduced by the loss of child support, she had a large tax bill with the i.r.s. breathing down her neck, and some accountant wants her to go to court.

She phoned Larry and they had a nice long talk about what was happening. He certainly did not want her to have all of these problems. As far as he was concerned, the divorce was done in a proper manner and he never foresaw the financial mess she was getting into after all these years. He advised her not to go to tax court, pay the i.r.s., get rid of her new accountant and begin to do a little budgeting.

Liz did as Larry recommended, but in order to pay the i.r.s. bill, she had to sell some securities. Since she was going to sell some stocks she might as well get some extra money to tide her over and help pay the college tuition for the four children in the upcoming semester. Liz sold a very large amount of stock. The stockbroker saw her coming and figured it was commission time, big time.

Liz paid off the i.r.s., put money down on the college tuition's and bought clothes for the family. As time went on that year she felt really smug that she had worked her way out of her financial mess. What Liz did not realize was that when she sold the securities two things were going to happen that never crossed her mind. First, she was going to receive less dividends, thus reducing her income even more and second, she never saved any of the money to cover the increase in taxes for the year due to the profit she made on the security sales. Liz's tailspin was going to continue.

What does this little story tell us about divorces and income taxes? There are eight tax and divorce implications in the story of Larry & Liz. If you were paying attention earlier in the chapter you would have known this. Let's take a look at what you missed.

1) Larry and Liz went to their family attorney. Regardless of how good he may be, there was the chance that he would not consider future tax implications for Liz. This he did not do. Because he was a family friend and confident, he overlooked the importance of thoroughly explaining important parts of the divorce. He probably assumed they understood.

2) Larry and Liz did a lot of excellent financial planning, but no matter how careful they were yesterday, there is always the chance that things can change materially in the future. New tax laws, new domestic issues and of course the impact of our ever changing society. These issues must be considered in a divorce.

3) When Liz received the real estate that was to be sold back to the corporations, the attorney should have had some type of schedules prepared to illustrate to Liz what was going to happen in the future when the payments started and the tax implications.

4) The attorney used the total dollar amount theory when he divided up the portion of alimony and child support. The biggest mistake made on this issue is that the child support ended at age 18 with no provisions for their college education.

5) Liz and Larry never really did sit down and review the divorce papers. The division of property seemed fair and that's about as far as the two of them read into the settlement. Divorce papers and especially the settlement should be read and studied. Always find out what you have and what you are going to get.

6) Liz and her accountant were way off the mark when they assumed that the dollars received on the installment sales were not taxable. It is true that property received in a divorce is tax free, but when that property is sold, no matter when or how, it becomes a taxable transaction. Interest received is also a taxable transaction.

7) A good tax accountant will not recommend that you as a client go to tax court. The only time you go to tax court is if you absolutely have to.

8) Whenever you find yourself selling securities to pay off the i.r.s., it is time to stand back and take a good look at your finances. I have seen clients begin selling income producing assets to pay off taxes or maybe some other type of bill and before long they find themselves in one heck of a pickle. It is the start of a very serious financial tailspin.

Here are a few good "one liners" to break up this boring stuff we just plowed through.

~~~~~~~~~~~~~~~~~~~~~~~~~~~~~~~~

The early bird may get the worm, but the second mouse gets the cheese.

If everything seems to be going well, you have obviously overlooked something.

Shin: A devise for finding furniture in the dark.

~~~~~~~~~~~~~~~~~~~~~~~~~~~~~~~~

Believe it or not, there are actually publications and some books on the market that tell us how to negotiate a "perfect" divorce. Before writing this chapter, I studied some of the suggestions for possible inclusion into my writings. Although I am sure there is such a thing as a "perfect" divorce settlement, my experience in practice has seen very little along lines of perfection.

The reason so many "perfect" divorce settlements go astray is that we live in an ever changing society. Parties to a divorce can never foresee the possible changes down the road. I personally have a hard time planning correctly for events happening three months away, let alone five years.

You have read throughout this book that it is so important to take the time to study, learn and calculate any and all financial arrangements. This is not only good tax and financial planning, but it will give you peace of mind. Not so much in what answers you come up with, but knowing that you are comfortable with the decision you make. Remember, you have to live with those decisions perhaps the rest of your life, so you had better be satisfied.

This chapter has dealt with taxable items in a divorce. There are situations where taxable alimony will not benefit either party. (This is part of the "perfect" settlement process.) The main theory behind the non-taxable alimony is that both parties are in the same income tax bracket and neither spouse would benefit. Another scenario is that the spouse who is paying the alimony is in a lower tax bracket than the receiving spouse. The payer spouse would have no tax benefit and the receiving spouse would not have to claim the alimony thus saving tax dollars. The theory behind this is that by not having to pay income taxes on the alimony, the receiving spouse could concede to a lower alimony payment. So far so good?

The only requirement for this type of settlement is that it has to be spelled out clearly in the divorce decree. This portion of the settlement has to be photocopied and attached to the tax return of the receiving spouse for each year the non-taxable alimony is in effect. Simple enough?

Now let's look at the real world. I personally would not recommend attaching anything personal to a tax return. Not in today's society and especially with the i.r.s. in such disarray. Next, I find that this theory does not take into consideration possible changes that might affect each of the parties involved. The payer spouse may have a job change or start up a new and successful business. At this point the payer is looking for tax deductions. The receiving spouse may be unable to work and the extra alimony might make the difference between just surviving and living comfortably.

There are so many theories, practices, laws and social considerations when it comes to divorce that it is very hard to come up with the right answers and conclusions. I've been interviewing clients for 60 years and I am still confused over what and how is the correct way to approach divorce settlements.

Unfortunately, most of my experience is seeing the client after the divorce has taken place and the damage has been done. Many clients try and go back to court and correct prior decisions and this doesn't always work. It is very time consuming and costly. The biggest cost is wear and tear on the human mind because you have to re-live this very difficult time all over again.

We can not end this chapter on a sour note so let's put in some good news about divorces to finish off the subject.

A divorced spouse, married for ten years or more, and who has not remarried, may collect on the ex-spouses Social Security at retirement age. This is a wonderful benefit, but there are some limitations. Check with the Social Security office and get the details.

Alimony may qualify as compensation and allow you to make an IRA contribution. If you are receiving taxable alimony, check with your tax adviser for more information.

The following story is a real play on words. I will not even attempt to pick a winner.

~~~~~~

An English professor wrote the words "woman without her man is nothing" on a blackboard and directed the students to punctuate it correctly.

The men wrote: "Woman without her man, is nothing."

The women wrote: "Women! Without her, man is nothing."

~~~~~~

INCOME TAX AUDITS
(You have been caught)

The number one fear of all taxpayers is getting audited. Every one of us has heard horror stories about i.r.s. audits and some of them are true, but most of them are highly exaggerated.

Regardless of the stories we hear, i.r.s. tax audits are a fact of life and we need to deal with them. First of all there is no set formula that creates a tax audit. Every year the i.r.s. sets up different audit flags which vary in different regions and are not constant from one year to another.

A good example of regional audit flags would be the problem they had in Las Vegas, Nevada. Several years ago the i.r.s. and the employees of the casinos were at odds over the classification of tips. The employees contended that tips were considered gifts from the patrons while the i.r.s. contended that the money received was tips, part of wages and fully taxable.

Even though it sounds like a silly reason not to pay taxes, the employees were dead serious and this rift went on for several years. The audit percentages in Las Vegas and other resort areas were way above the normal range. For your information, the i.r.s. won the war. Even I have to admit they were right.

A TAXPAYER'S NIGHTMARE

Certain tax return items will trigger an audit every time and this is what I have listed below:

1) Not filing a tax return, especially when you have 1099 or W-2 income.

2) Not reporting all of your income! i.r.s. computers match up all W-2's - 1099's - Partnership Returns - Real Estate Transactions and stock Transactions with amounts reported on your return and they had better match or else!

3) High expenses and low income.

4) Excessive deductions well above the norm. (What ever that is).

5) Math errors. (This is the #1 problem on tax returns).

6) Incomplete returns. (This is the second biggest problem on tax returns).

Most audit notices from the i.r.s. are computer generated and are not really audits. Something on the tax return did not match up or some items need to be verified. These notices constitute about 80% of the so called audits you hear about.

If you received one of these computer generated questionnaires always answer it promptly. If you owe a few extra dollars because of an addition error or you forgot to include some income, verify their amount and if it is correct, send them a check. They will be happy and, end of audit.

When the notice informs you that information is missing from your return or they want to verify a dependent, need a Social Security number, whatever, answer the notice and mail it back. Again this will be the end of the audit.

OK, none of the above applies and they want to see you and your records in person. Now we have an audit and the circus is about to begin. What do you do when you receive a notice like this?

1) Yell at the spouse and the kids?

2) Kick the dog or cat?
3) Sit down and have a drink? (Two is better)
4) All of the above? (Most likely)

Before we get into audit procedures and before you fall asleep, let's talk about i.r.s. auditors. These people are a mixed box of puppies to say the least. The education level of i.r.s. employees range from no education to the whiz kid who is an attorney with MBA, CPA, and three other funny looking symbols behind their name.

For some reason it seems that when you phone the i.r.s., you always seem to be talking with the employee with no education. Right? They don't make sense and you already dislike them on general principles. In my 60 years, I have really come across some doozies. In the years past, these people did not have to give their names or employee number. Now at least you can find out the name of the person you are talking at. The proper English would be "talking with" only it always seems to be a one way conversation. You are asking the questions and the other end of the phone is saying, "I can't tell you that", "We are not allowed to give legal advice" and the clincher is, "I will need to talk to my supervisor on this matter". Why didn't a supervisor answer the phone to begin with, since they are the only ones who can answer a question?

The other day I phoned the i.r.s. to find out the status of a client's file. A nice voice came on the line and said that all representatives were busy and there would be a six minute delay. A few minutes passed and the same nice voice came on and said there would be a nine minute delay. I thought we were going backwards, but this was the i.r.s. and these things happen. About ten minutes later the nice voice came on and said the delay was only about three minutes and thanked me for my patience. About another ten minutes went by and another, not so nice voice, said that I had been disconnected and to please call back at a time when they were not as busy. I was not a happy person when that message came on.

Getting back to the education levels of i.r.s. auditors, I can only give them in general terms as I am not into i.r.s policies. For simplicity, we will assume there are four levels of i.r.s. auditors.

1) In house Auditors. These people do all of the general duties relating to standard procedures and practices. The education level is normally a college degree in accounting and/or business. This is actually the starting position with the i.r.s.

2) Field Auditors. Field auditors go out in the real world and cause havoc. They audit individuals and businesses, normally at the taxpayers place or at their tax adviser's office. These auditors are well versed in their field and know their business. The education level for these people are all college graduates with some MBA's and CPA's in the group. This is the dangerous category of auditors. Some of these people are not only sharp in their knowledge, but with experience, develop a canny knack for throwing taxpayers off the mark to get additional information out of them. It is always best to have your tax adviser deal with these auditors. Believe me when I say the cat and mouse game starts here.

This is also the category of auditors that you read about, especially during the past Senate Hearings on the i.r.s. Although they are loaded with education, backed by unfair tax laws, they still go out of their way to make it hard on individuals and businesses. I guess we can call them middle management. They are always trying to make their mark and get promoted or earn a bonus. Dealing with these people is a real experience.

3) Tax Fraud Auditors. This is the cream of the crop. They are out looking for audit items that constitute criminal fraud. When these auditors come to visit you, there is really a problem in the works.

I have never had the pleasure of their company and neither have any of my clients. The only thing I know about them is what I read in newsletters and i.r.s. horror stories. The education level of these auditors can include, but is not limited to: CPA's, MBA's and attorneys, each with a whole bunch of funny symbols behind their names.

In most audit cases, you may be represented by a tax adviser or an attorney. In tax fraud cases you should always be represented by a criminal lawyer. Never talk to an i.r.s. tax fraud auditor on your own. Always have your attorney present and let him do all the talking and negotiating. These auditors are not easy to work with. They have more tricks up their sleeve than any magician.

4)   Appeals Division Auditors. This group is not really in the audit business. They are all past auditors that have been moved up to management. Their job is to hear cases that have been disputed or unsolved. Their main purpose is to settle as many cases as possible before the situation is taken to tax court. Even the i.r.s. doesn't want to go to tax court. No one wins in tax court but the lawyers.

I have worked with many appeals officers and have always found them to be pleasant, cooperative and very forgiving. They accomplish their mission by giving the taxpayer every benefit possible, so long as the case can be resolved right there in the office.

I have listed just four auditor classifications. Knowing the i.r.s., they probably have 4,000 classifications. I listed just the four to give you a general idea of what auditors are all about. I hope none of you readers ever have the opportunity to meet one!
When you receive an audit notice, and you had your taxes prepared by someone, contact them immediately. If it is one of those computer generated notices asking questions or stipulating some income items were omitted, contact your tax adviser. Remember that in one year alone, the i.r.s. sent out 5,000,000 incorrect tax delinquency notices, so you may have received one. If you prepared your own tax return, review the return to see if they are correct. DO NOT assume they are correct.

If it is not a computer generated notice it will probably start out something like this. "Your return has been selected for further review by the internal revenue service" "Please call the above telephone number to set up an appointment." "We will need the following information-------". Now we have an audit in process!!

There are several basic procedures in preparing for an audit. If you know what the i.r.s. is looking for, it would be very simple, but in most cases you will not have the slightest idea. The following list will give you an idea of what to do:

1) Review the tax return that is in question. Look for anything that may be out of line such as overlooked income or an error in your itemized deductions.

2) Collect and review all of your paperwork, W-2's and 1099's. If you itemized deductions you most likely will have mortgage interest and real estate taxes. Be sure that the amounts on your return agree with the 1098 forms sent to you from the mortgage company.

3) If you have rental property and there was a large amount of repairs, check the invoices and be sure that the repairs were of a temporary nature and no large amount was spent on improvements. One of the most common errors on a rental return is where capital improvements are written off as repairs. For a general explanation of capital improvements, I will list the most common ones:

    A) New roof or a major expenditure for
        replacement parts and sealing.
    B) Large plumbing bills for new pipes and
        various plumbing fixtures.
    C) Large electrical bills for rewiring or to
        bring the building up to code.
    D) Landscaping other than plants & shrubs.
        Sprinkler systems are not an expense.
    E) Painting the building to make it more attractive.
    F) Touch up after a renter moves out is an expense.

4) Review any transactions where stocks or other types of property were sold. Be sure your cost basis and dates of purchase and sale are correct.

5) Business income and expenses. This is a favorite target for the i.r.s. Review items on the return with your bookkeeper and be sure they can be substantiated. Carefully review your travel and entertainment expenses. This is the area most taxpayers cheat on and the i.r.s. know this.

6) Employee business expenses. Just as in a business, carefully review your travel / entertainment expenses. Document all of your travels and appointment dates with customers.

7) Child Care Expenses and the Earned Income Credit are being targeted by the i.r.s. almost as much as travel and entertainment. A lot of people out there have been cheating for years in these areas and the i.r.s. is having a great success rate on audits.

While you are reviewing your return, put your supporting documents in separate envelopes for each item reviewed. When the auditor ask questions you can whip out the receipts as proof. Auditors hate this because you beat them to the punch, but the audit goes along very smoothly and will end a lot faster.

If you are missing any documents, find them and do it as soon as you can. Sometimes things get lost and to wait until the last minute will cause you a bunch of grief. Remember, an audit is a very serious matter and it should get all of your attention until you feel comfortable about your tax return. You had better know more than the auditor when the meeting begins.

Let's take a break from the heavy stuff. Did you know that:

If Barbie was life size, her measurements would be 39-23-33?

Winston Churchill was born in a ladies rest room during a dance?

In most advertisements, including newspapers, the time displayed on a watch is 10:10?

Now that you have all of your records put together and you feel good about your return, what next? Well, we should back up a bit. First of all I do not recommend any taxpayer representing himself at an audit. Remember that the i.r.s. will not audit your return unless they know something you don't. They are not going to audit an individual with only wages. The audits are generally directed at taxpayers with outside income, various expenses, or a complicated return.

Because it was a complicated return, you probably had someone prepare it for you. Have the person who prepared your return represent you before the i.r.s. If you used one of those new fancy computer programs and you did it yourself, you have my condolences. None the less, you should find someone to represent you before the i.r.s.

Why is it so important to have someone represent you during an audit? If you were paying attention a few pages ago you would remember that the i.r.s. field auditors have a bunch of tricks up their sleeves and know how to intimidate taxpayers. You always want to have a buffer between you and the auditor.

Never have the audit at your residence or place of business. Always have it at your tax adviser's office or at the i.r.s. offices. Why?? You do not want them to see or analyze your lifestyle. This may sound a little silly to you, but believe me when I say they are looking for something and you do not want to help them in any way except for the items they ask for. You have the legal obligation to work with them, but not for them.

The recommended audit procedures are as follows:

Always have a tax adviser with you and let them do the talking. If this is not possible and you go it alone:

1) Answer all questions to the best of your knowledge. Always be cooperative and pleasant. The auditor has a job to do and alienating them is not in your best interest.

2) Never volunteer information! Answer all questions as short as possible. If one seems out of line or can be embarrassing to you, simply say "I will get back to you on that question". You have a legal right to do this. Don't let the auditor tell you different!

3) Under all circumstances, keep your cool. Some i.r.s. auditors are very experienced at ruffling taxpayer's feathers. They do this to

throw you off base and get the upper hand in negotiations. They know you will make a mistake and they will jump all over it.

4) Do not underestimate the auditor. Some of these people are very well educated and become masters at their trade. Each auditor has their own method to "Open you Up". Some are overly friendly while others are very vague in their questions. Each one has their own purpose and methods.

5) Be very careful in what and how you say something. Always watch for where the conversation is going. Each thing you say can open new doors for the auditor. Always keep the conversation on the topic at hand.

6) Remember auditors are not there for your benefit. They were sent there to find additional tax dollars for the i.r.s. kitty. They all have the feeling that you have their money in your pocket!

7) If you and the auditor can not come to a conclusion of the audit, ask for more time to find the answers. Sometimes it is best to make another appointment. The audit does not have to be completed at one sitting. The main thing to accomplish is that the audit is moving in the right direction and a solution is in sight. Always leave on a positive note.

Now would be a good time to relate another i.r.s. horror story. This is a true story that happened to me. It is not really a horror story, in fact it is kind of comical.

I received a phone call from one of my clients whose aunt was in a mess with the i.r.s. She did about everything possible to ruffle the i.r.s. office and they were about to lower the boom on her. She was in her 80's and wanted no part of the government. Her tax adviser tried for years to keep her out of trouble and finally decided to quit her case.

I met with the lady and she lowered the boom on me. She described her problems with the i.r.s. with as many four letter words as I can ever remember hearing from a lady. I reviewed her tax return and it seemed to be properly prepared. The problem started when I asked her if she could verify all of her expenses on the rental property that was in question.

She said that she had every receipt, but it was none of the government's business to see them. After all, she had been filing tax returns for over 60 years and they should know this and they should know that, etc. and so on. Well folks, I had a challenge at hand.

We talked for a while, or I should say she talked and I listened for a while, but I finally got my message through. She agreed to provide records if I had the auditor meet me at my house, which was also my office. We worked out the details of what was needed and that I would set the audit up for about three weeks away.

I phoned the i.r.s. and set up the appointment. I talked to the client three or four times, answering questions and helped her get vital information. No problem! She was most cooperative and said that the records would be at my office two days before the auditor was to be there. When the appointed day for the records to arrive came, she never showed up. I phoned her and she said she was just finishing and I would have them the next day. The next day came and went and I still did not have the records.

Finally, the nephew showed up with her boxes of records two hours before the audit. Inside the boxes were paper bags, shoe boxes and tin cans full of receipts and lord knows what else. I was one livid tax accountant! I phoned the little old lady and read her the riot act. She listened to me and when I was finished she calmly replied, "It is nice to see that you have some spunk young man". "Remember, they just said they wanted to see my records and you have them all so what more do you expect me to do?". Well I had to laugh. There was nothing else to do. My wife thought this was the funniest thing she ever saw. She had always heard of people putting records, money and jewelry in shoe boxes and tin cans, and now she finally met one.

Since the audit was only an hour away, I couldn't cancel so I was stuck with some i.r.s. auditor and a box full of records. I went through the boxes and bags to get some idea of what was in there. Nothing made sense and there was no order in which the records were stored. I assume that whatever container was handy was where the receipt ended up.

At ten o'clock the auditor showed up. We exchanged pleasantries and I had her sit at the dining room table where there was plenty of room to spread out. I told her of the mess she faced and apologized for the condition of the records. She seemed to understand as the little old lady's file was probably full of comments from other auditor's notes.

The auditor sat at the table for about two hours shuffling papers. I checked in with her from time to time to see if there was anything I could do. About 12:30 she came into my office and said she was finished. Due to the condition of the records she was unable to make out a full report, but she did some spot testing and found that the receipts she needed were there and this would satisfy the investigation. The return would be accepted as filed.

I signed off on the papers she had and the auditor left. My wife came into my office and told me what actually happened. My wife was in the kitchen making cookies so she had a full view of the auditor in the dining room. The auditor shuffled through a few receipts, wrote something down, grumbled and then got some more receipts. This process went on for the full 2½ hours. There was no way in the world she could have come to some conclusion with the records I presented her. If she did any kind of an audit, it would have taken her 3 to 5 days and I doubt that it would be very complete.

I phoned my little old lady and told her the good news. All she said to me was "You learned something today young man. Keep this in mind for your clients in future audits. It works every time!" Who am I to argue with a sweet little old lady when it comes to the i.r.s.?

Before we get into another story about i.r.s. auditors, let's look at some humor. I love stories about what kids say and think.

"Never trust a dog to watch your food"
Patrick, age 10

"Never try to hide a piece of broccoli in
a glass of milk" - Rosemary, age 7

"Never try to baptize a cat"
Laura, age 10

"Never spit when on a roller coaster"
Scott, age 10

"Stay away from prunes"
Randy, age 9

Answers given by 2nd grade school children to the following questions:

Why did God make mothers?
- She's the only one who knows where the scotch tape is.
- Mostly to clean the house.
- To help us get out of there when we were getting born.

How did God make mothers?
- He used dirt, just like for the rest of us.
- Magic, plus super powers …. And a lot of stirring.
- God made my mom just the same like he made me. He just used bigger parts.

What ingredients are mothers made of?
- God makes mothers out of clouds and angel hair and everything nice in the world, plus one dab of mean.
- They had to get their start from men's bones. Then they mostly used string, I think.

Why did God give you your mother and not some other mom?
- We're related.

- God knew she likes me a lot more than other people's mom like me.

What kind of a little girl was your mom?
- My mom has always been my mom and none of that other stuff.
- I don't know because I wasn't there, but my guess would be she was pretty bossy.
- They say she used to be nice.

What did mom need to know about your dad before she married him?
- His last name
- She had to know his background. Like is he a crook? Does he get drunk on beer?
- Does he make at least $800 a year? Did he say NO to drugs and YES to chores?

Why did your mom marry your dad?
- My dad makes the best spaghetti in the world and my mom EATS A LOT!
- She got too old to do anything else with him.
- My grandma says that mom didn't have her thinking cap on.

Who's the boss at your house?
- Mom doesn't want to be the boss, but she has to because dad's such a goof ball.
- Mom. You can tell by room inspection. She sees the stuff under the bed.
- I guess mom is, but only because she has a lot more to do than dad.

What's the difference between moms and dads?
- Moms work at work and work at home. Dads just go to work at work.
- Moms know how to talk to teachers without scaring them.
- Dads are taller and stronger, but moms have all the real power cause that's who you got to ask if you want to sleep over at your friends.
- Moms have magic. They make you feel better without medicine.

What does your mom do in her spare time?
- Mothers don't do spare time.
- To hear her tell it, she pays bills all day long.

What would it take to make your mom perfect?
- On the inside she's already perfect. Outside, I think some kind of plastic surgery.
- Diet. You know, her hair. I'd diet ---- maybe blue.

If you could change one thing about your mom, what would it be??

She has this weird thing about me keeping my room clean. I'd get rid of that. I'd make my mom smarter. Then she would know it was my sister who did it and not me! I would like for her to get rid of those invisible eyes on the back of her head.

ARE YOU SURE THIS IS
PART OF THE AUDIT?

TAXES AND YOUR BUSINESS
(An audit waiting to happen)

When it comes to businesses, we have to approach taxes from another whole viewpoint. Your chance of getting audited will increase about 100%. Scary as it may sound, it one of the facts of life we have to face.

Why are small businesses getting audited more and more each year? I don't believe there is anything in print, but the i.r.s. knows the chance for error is greater in a business and the possibility of finding tax dollars is more likely.

One fact that is overlooked by most people is that there are two taxes related to businesses. One of course is the income tax, but the one most of us forget is the Social Security tax. Some profitable business owners pay no income tax because they have non business writeoffs that offset income, but all profitable business owners must pay Social Security taxes. Since Uncle Sam has to borrow from the Social Security fund in order to exist, they zero in on businesses looking for profit in any way they can.

I do not plan on giving you a lesson in business accounting and taxation. First of all, you wouldn't listen to me and I don't really need a second reason.

This section will cover a few tricks of the trade and I will also try and give business owners some food for thought that may keep you out of trouble with the i.r.s. (Yeah, good luck Carey)

One of the most foolish things business people do is not keep receipts. I tell all of my clients that every $100 in receipts they miss will cost them a minimum of $30.00 in taxes. Now, how did I come up with that figure? It is a simple computation that should be implanted in all business owner's minds. Minimum tax rate is 15% and Social Security tax is another 15%.

Now let's look at it from another viewpoint. To make a $30.00 profit on an investment, after taxes, you have to make one heck of lot more than $100. What I'm saying is that it is easier to save $30.00 than it is to make $30.00 when it come to business transactions, especially when all you have to do is keep those little pieces of paper that get all crumbled up in your pocket.

There are two types of tax accounting that can apply to businesses. One is "Cash Basis Accounting" and the other is "Accrual Basis Accounting"

Cash Basis Accounting records only the money you receive and the money actually spent in a tax year, regardless of when the income was earned or the expense incurred. Your bank statement and some cash receipts constitute your whole accounting system. A credit card expense is also considered a cash payment because you are legally liable for the debt according to tax law.

I recommend "Cash Basis Accounting" for small service oriented businesses. Most proprietors don't really care about sophisticated accounting procedures.
"How much did I get and how much did I spend" is the basic motto for small businesses.

Accrual Basis Accounting is more complicated and gives the business owner a better picture of his business performance. Here we include, within a tax year, all of the money "earned", (regardless of when it was received), and all of the expenses "incurred", (regardless of when the expense was paid). We do this with accounts called "Receivables" and "Payables"

Accounts Receivable is money due you, but not yet collected, while Accounts Payable is money you owe for operating expenses, but not yet paid. This vehicle puts your complete operation within a twelve month period, (tax year), and you will know exactly what you have accomplished in a given period. This type of accounting procedure costs more money and certainly is more complicated.

I recommend Accrual Basis Accounting for almost all businesses. First, it gives you a better picture of your operation and second, it will level out your income tax bill over a period of years. There is one catch to all of this and that is you have to make a determination on your first business tax return as to which accounting basis you are going to use. Once you make that choice you are stuck with it forever. There are ways to change your basis, but it is not easy and not recommended by most accountants.

There are three basic forms of business ownership.

Sole proprietorship (One owner). For tax purposes the owner files a "Schedule C" within the personal tax return and combines the business with other income received that year. Business earnings are subject to Social Security Taxes and paid along with other taxes due.

Partnership (Two or more owners). For tax purposes, the partnership keeps a complete set of books, files a separate tax return and gives the owners a "Schedule K" at year end that serves the same purpose as a W-2, only much more complicated. The numbers on the "Schedule K" are placed on various lines of the 1040 tax return according to their classification. If the owner materially participates in the partnership, their earnings are subject to Social Security Taxes and paid along with other taxes due.

Corporations. There are two types of corporations for tax purposes. One is an "S Corporation" and the tax implications are very much like a partnership. The other is a "C Corporation" and it is a completely separate tax entity. The "C"corporation files a tax return and pays taxes based on the return. All earnings to the participating owners are put on a W-2 form as wages. Social Security Taxes are taken out of the wages, just like any other employee.

The above is a real simple explanation of business ownership and the tax implications. For those who need to make a decision on which form of business is best suited for you, please see a tax adviser or attorney.

Depreciation will not be discussed here due to the high technical nature. I do not recommend the average taxpayer trying to figure it out, even with a computer tax program.

Remember that inventory items are not an expense when you purchase them. It is an asset until sold. Careful accounting of inventory is essential.

One item I have seen on many tax returns for businesses is "Miscellaneous Expenses" of $5,000 or more. Well, there is no such thing as $5,000 of miscellaneous expenses. Every expense has a category and should be listed separately. Not only is this improper accounting, but it is a definite red flag to the i.r.s. If you cannot find a category for all that money, I guarantee you an auditor will.

Auto expenses can be listed as actual expenses incurred, (ie. gas, repairs, interest, depreciation, insurance, etc.), or can be listed as mileage driven times the i.r.s. mileage rate which is around 55 cents per mile. This is a tough one. I work my clients on a case by case basis because you can benefit in so many different ways. If you lease a car for business, you are compelled to use actual expenses.

When making bank deposits to a business account, it is a must that you separate income items from loans, insurance proceeds, and especially any owner contributions. When you are having an i.r.s. audit, the bank statement is the main focal point. To the i.r.s., all deposits are income and nothing else counts. Please take the time to list the source of each deposit.

Travel, meals and entertainment have always been a high priority in the audit area. Be sure you separate travel and lodging, (100% deductible), from food, drinks and entertainment, (50% deductible). It is very important that each credit card charge be analyzed. If you stay at a hotel and charge your meals to your room, be sure to separate meals, etc from lodging. If you don't, the i.r.s. will be happy to do it for you.

A lot of clients ask me about meals for employees. The simple answer is that if the meals are provided to the employees for the convenience of the employer, such as a restaurant providing meals for their employees to keep them on the premises, then it is income tax free to the employee and tax deductible for the employer.

Social Security taxes have to be taken out on the employee's paycheck by a formula fair to all.

A party for employees is 100% deductible, while a party for customers/clients is only 50% deductible. If you entertain customers at your home, be sure to keep all of the receipts as this can be a deductible expense.

You will have to document the reason for the party and its business relationship. (You can not deduct the cost of your spouse's labor. Sorry!)

Are you bored yet? Here is some light stuff.

~~~~~~~~~~~~~~~~~~~~~~~~~~~~~~~
A clothes dryer is an appliance designed to to eat socks.

Eternity: Last two minutes of a football game

PUT IT IN THE BANK!

PUT IT IN YOUR POCKET

Let's talk about reporting income. Of course everyone is honest and the thought of slipping a few bucks in your pocket never occurred to you? Well, I sure don't buy that and neither does the i.r.s. Believe me, they are always looking for money that might just fall into the cracks of life.

I tell all of my clients "Report all income, it just isn't worth the hassle. If you are pocketing money from your business, don't tell me about it". Accountant/Client relationships are not like Attorney/Client relationships. I will always take every deduction possible for my clients whether they be gray, white or black. I will not cheat for one of my clients. Believe it or not, they like my answer.

I am a firm believer that money should be made from whatever endeavor you choose, but not from income taxes. Always try to save money on income taxes, not make money.

One area of business not necessarily relating to taxes, but very important to me, is the use of "Sub Contract Labor", "Casual Labor" or "Paying Wages Under The Table". Well folks, this is a NO-NO!!

A sub contractor is a person doing work for you as a separate entity. A sub contractor is normally licensed to do business and works for or with many customers. Work is done to your specifications, but at their convenience, expertise and with no direct supervision. This does not fit the bill of someone working in your plant, office or shop.

There is a 20 point test used by the i.r.s. And most state agencies for classifying workers. All business people should be familiar with this test. Another fact that you will have to realize is that Federal rules and State rules are very different when it comes to sub contract work.

If you are a business that pays your employees as subcontractors you are putting yourself in a very dangerous position with great legal and tax consequences, not so much income taxes, but payroll taxes. This problem is not brought about by the Ir.'s., but by the state governments. That piece of paper you have them sign as subcontractors is useless.

Recently, the i.r.s. has relaxed some of the laws that relate to how employees are classified, but in general, anyone working for you, under your supervision, all day and almost everyday is an employee. Period. End!!

How do employers get caught paying workers under the table with no deductions? Well there are five ways to get caught and I have seen them all happen too many times.

1) Worker gets hurt on the job. Because they are not listed as an employee, they will not be able to collect worker's compensation insurance or disability insurance.

2) Worker is laid off, quits or is fired. Because they are not listed as an employee, they can not collect unemployment insurance.

3) Worker and boss have a falling out. The worker can report you to the labor commission. This is really a bad one to get involved with.

4) Worker receiving a 1099 form at year end with no income taxes paid, will be hurt at tax time and will want revenge.

5) There is also a chance for a random outside audit that will uncover wages being paid as sub contract work.

These five simple examples would scare the heck out of me if I was an employer. What happens if you are caught paying wages as sub contract work? First of all, you will be open for audit of all wages paid for a period up to three years, maybe more. Next the state or federal agency, (probably both), will bill you for all unreported payroll taxes for the period under audit. How much will that be? Let's make a few simple calculations based on $3,000 per year in wages for three years.

Total wages paid:	$9,000.00
Social Security @ 15.3%	$1,377.00
Federal Unemp. Ins. @ .08%	72.00
Federal Income Taxes @15%	1,350.00
State Unempl. Ins. @ 3.5%	315.00
State Income Taxes @ 5%	450.00
Total taxes due	$3,114.00

Now this is only a tax bill. It does not include penalties and interest. Add another 10% or more and your piggy bank just shrank. Still think hiding wages is a good business decision?

I have seen tax bills get up to $25,000. Believe me when I say the employer made a few changes and quick.

I have always told everyone, including relatives, friends and business clients not to pay wages under the table. How many listened? Very few. I hear the same thing over and over again. "Well Joe told me this and Sam told me that". My standard answer to such stupidity is, "Have Joe or Sam prepare your tax returns." That wrinkles a few feathers, but they know I am dead serious.

When you have a business, take the time and spend the money to have some professionals guide you in making the very difficult decisions that come with the territory. I do a lot of consulting work, more now than before, because I am semi-retired and do not want to work the long hours required by accounting practices.

People come to me and for less than $200.00 can find out more about business practices and shortcuts than they ever imagined. If you go to a consultant with a prepared, thought out list of questions and/or problems, they can help you solve these situations in just a couple of hours time. This time frame may not answer all of the questions you have, but believe me you will have benefited to the tune of $1,000 or more in business and tax savings alone. To me that is a good investment. I'll spend $200.00 to make a $1,000.00 every day of the week. Besides, we consultants need the money!

I have a lot of business horror stories, but I prefer not to write about them. Why? I feel everyone who wants to go into business, and can afford to, should give it a try. It is one of our true "American Dreams"

When you mention that you want to go into business for yourself, at least 80% of the people you talk with will try and discourage you. Why do they do this? Are they smarter than you? No, they haven't got the guts to try it themselves. Believe me when I say it takes a lot of guts to go into business. A lot of young people go into business for themselves and a lot of those youngsters fail. They don't care. They just go out and do it all over again. These younger folks have no fears and everything in life is a game.

When the years start to pass before our eyes, we have a tendency to become more cautious and undoubtedly we have assumed more responsibility. A decision to go into business at a later age is more difficult due to family obligations and the such. But, for some people the desire to own a business is so great that it will happen sooner or later.

I have been self employed all of my life. Sometimes I had to work for other people, for a while, to pick up slack in the finances. But that never lasted very long, as I was going to be self employed no matter what.

If you make a decision to go into business, my advice to you is to go slow. If you have a job, do not quit! If possible, run your business on the side and take advantage of the guaranteed paycheck as long as you can. When you find that your new business can support you and the family, then weigh the decision to quit your job. The first couple of years in any business are tough and additional income never hurt anyone.

Over the years I have given out so much advice that it scares me. I often wonder how I know so much and begin to doubt myself. I guess we all have these feelings. I have spent my whole life in the business world. I learned though experience and the school of hard knocks. I read a lot about business and love to explore new ideas. Right now I'm into cyberspace and the newest internet technology.

During the first 30 years of my business life, we had to do everything by hand. Now we have computers. I can accomplish more in one hour today than I could in eight hours 15 years ago. The world of business and even life has changed dramatically. We are no longer a separate society on earth. All forms of business and life are now on a global scale and the possibilities are endless.

When I talk to the younger generation about schooling and the future, computers always come to mind. When there is a doubt about which field to go into, I always recommend computer technology. You can become a doctor, lawyer, dentist or engineer. You can become an accountant, social worker or scientist. No matter what field you choose, be sure that you are highly versed in computer technology and then apply that technology to your field of endeavor. I sincerely believe that we have only just begun when it comes to the value of computers.

While writing the business section of this book, I was thinking about giving business owners a good tax tip. I scratched by head many times trying to remember some of the best advice I have ever given. When I came down to the final selection, I found that it was not necessarily advice on taxes, but a business decision that must be made by all small business owners.

When the tax year ends and all of the records go to the accountant, most of us kind of forget the past year and start concentrating on the up coming year.

We have worked all year trying to make a living or at least make ends meet. Now we ask the accountant to take all of the numbers and with their magical pencil rearrange the numbers so there will be little or no taxes to pay. This is good thinking and in many cases the accountant can help you out quite a bit. But is it the right decision?

One of the most important things business owners overlook is the fact that at one time or another you are going to try and get a loan. This could be a business loan, home loan or an investment loan. The purpose is immaterial, but the fact is you have to qualify for the loan. Because you are self employed the lender will want to see your tax return for at least three years to analyze your ability to pay. Where do they look? At the Schedule "C" that list your business activities.

If every year you show little or no profit, you won't get the loan. I have seen business owners talk their heads off trying to explain the bottom line to a banker. The banker may understand what you are talking about, but he doesn't really care. He has a committee to answer to and the committee only looks at numbers. Believe me when I say the personal approach to banking is long gone. Banks and lenders are bottom line oriented and each year it gets harder and harder to obtain financing.

OK, so what is the great advice we are going to receive? Show a profit and pay taxes? You're crazy Carey, Uncle Sam is not going to get any more money out of me than what is absolutely necessary!

My advice is exactly that. Show a profit each year and pay taxes on the income. This will be one of your best investment for the coming years.

I know we can't argue through a book, so I will lay the facts of life out for you. If you finish this book, you might even end up agreeing with me.

The first thing to consider is that life is full of uncertainties. None of us can predict the future. If we could, there would be a whole bunch of little Bill Gates running around. We have to prepare ourselves for the many adversities we are going to face.

Aside from medical problems, which is normally the number one drawback, we have to consider retirement. Retirement is not a drawback, but it will come to all of us and we had better be prepared.

Most business owners say they will set up a retirement account and the hell with Social Security. Most young people do not believe that Social Security will be there when they retire. Well, this type of thinking is ridiculous.

Social Security has a lot of problems. The government has screwed up the fund since the day it was designed some 60 plus years ago. These problems can be and will be resolved. The government can't do it, so they will look outside the government for help. They will never privatize Social Security, but business experts, from all phases of life, will step in and get it back on track again.

Every year, when I interview my business clients, I always ask the same question. Did you set up your retirement account and how is it going? At least 50%, maybe more, did not set up a retirement account. If they already had one, they didn't contribute to it and did not plan to by April 15th.

I talk to other tax accountants about this and they have a similar experience. Unless people are forced to save, they won't. Based on my past experience with clients, most of them are going to have to rely on Social Security for their retirement years.

Getting back to showing a profit each year, I tell my clients that if they do not show a profit, they won't be paying into the Social Security Fund and there won't be any retirement dollars when the time comes. Some agree with me and some don't. I can't change their minds, but I am always trying.

Considering the facts about loans and Social Security might help taxpayers understand why my advice on showing a profit makes sense. I don't want anyone to pay more taxes than necessary. I have spent my entire career fighting the inequities of taxation. But, sometimes it is necessary to spend money to make money, and planning for your retirement is money well spent.

I wrote a book about 20 years ago when I first retired. Speaking of retiring, I've retired so many times in my career, I never know if I'm retired or still working. Anyway, this book was written about starting a business with all of the shortcuts, tax tips and pitfalls I could possibly think of to help people go into business.

Well folks, our tax laws, business practices and economy changed so quickly, my book was outdated before it was ever published. I rewrote the book several times and it was still outdated, so I quit. I bring this up only as a reminder to all of you that we live in an ever changing environment and it is going to change even more and each change will come faster than the year before.

The only true advice I can give to any business person is to accept the changes, enjoy the benefits, and never stop trying.

A couple more good ones:

~~~~~~~~~~~~~~~~~~~~~~~~~~~~~~

3 out of 4 Americans make up 75% of the population.

43% of all statistics are worthless (see above)

~~~~~~~~~~~~~~~~~~~~~~~~~~~~~~~~~~~

New Wrinkles From The I.R.S.
(What will be next?)

The i.r.s. is always claiming they are short handed in personnel. Well, if any of them worked a full day they could fire ½ of their staff. Over the last few years they hired 9,000 new auditors and still claim to be shorthanded. So they are starting some new wrinkles as described below.

One of the new wrinkles is that they are now sending out audits by mail telling the tax payer that they have deductions not allowed by the i.r.s.

If the taxpayer disagrees, they recommend you go to tax court. Now this is heavy. A mail audit to tax court scares the hell out of every taxpayer who gets this notice. Aren't there many steps in between?

Well this is the new wrinkle, scare the taxpayers into paying without further to do. Not my clients !!!!!!!

We always answer the mail audit with more questions then Carter has pills. They don't like this, but we do get their attention and slow them down.

Another new trick they are using is stating they never got the information you sent them. I have a client who sent the requested information by Fed Ex, signed receipt requested. We got the signed receipt, but they still claim they never received it and have no knowledge of the employee who sign the receipt.

Now, ladies and gentlemen, someone is fibbing here !!

I deal with the Tax Advocate's office all of the time. They told me not to send anything to them as it gets lost. Send all info by fax. So one of my clients faxed them 35 pages of a travel log and all receipts for travel and entertainment, another 10 sheets. Can you imagine how long that took?

Well, as usual, they never got the fax. Can you believe I have one ticked off client who said some naughty naughty words?????

This year I did something I thought I would never do in my 60 years of tax practice. I asked the i.r.s. to physically audit one of my clients in their field office. Now how many people ask for an audit?

Well, this really threw them a curve and they have not answered me yet. They probably think I've lost it and maybe I have, but how else can you settle a tax problem that has been going on for over two years?

THE LAST CHAPTER
(Yippee, it is almost over)

I have really enjoyed writing this book. I know how painful it must have been for some readers. Taxes are not the favorite subject of most Americans. They are part of our lives and some understanding of the issues is very important.

One of the most rewarding things in a person's life is to know that you have been able to help friends and clients. I have had two full accounting practices over the years. The first one was in the San Francisco/Bay Area. I practiced there for 20 years before I sold. I had to sign a covenant not to compete as part of the sale, so I was not able to keep any of the clients I worked with for those 20 years.

My second practice was started in Incline Village, Nevada. Although I have moved several times, I still have most of the original clients from that area and Northern Nevada. I feel very fortunate to have these clients stay with me.

Now that we are in the age of advanced telecommunications, I have been able to expand my practice over seven states. With the advent of fax machines and computers, my clients are only a click away. I always converse with my clients several times a year so we are in constant contact.

Since the very first day I went into practice, my clients have always been some of my best friends. We have developed a rapport that is very, very special. I care about every one of them and they know this. My decisions on their tax returns have always been for their benefit. Sometimes I had them pay more taxes than the next accountant would have, but it was done with their best interest in mind.

I went to a class reunion a few months ago. While I was in the area, I set up golf dates with all my old pals. Many of my ex-clients in the area came up to me at one time or another and thanked me for the years I worked with them. That was very special to me and made me think that "Hey, I did OK".

I plan to continue doing taxes as long as I'm able. My other business activities have wound down and this is good. I need to play more golf, bowl more often and chase those silly fish around the many ponds in this area. When I fish, I couldn't care less if I caught one. Just to have the opportunity to sit out in the middle of nowhere and reflect upon life is all the relaxation and enjoyment I need.

One thing that I have learned in life and it might be something for you to think about and that it is:

~~~~~~~~~~~~~~~~~~~~~~~~~~~~

Some days you're the dog, and some days you're the fire hydrant.

~~~~~~~~~~~~~~~~~~~~~~~~~~~~

THE I.R.S. LOSES
(We Whipped Them Big Time)

In the chapter on tax audits, I mentioned that I was in the middle of an audit and because it had not been finalized I could not discuss the case.

The other day I received the final audit papers and now I can include the audit as part of this book. It took about 13 months to complete and with a lot of patience, planning and a few tricks of the trade, it had a very happy ending.

This audit was a combination of every i.r.s. horror story I included in this book, and then some. This audit included 90% of what you read about during the Senate I.R.S. Reform Hearings. We had it all.

The taxpayers were not clients of mine. They were referred to me by a friend. The taxpayers had been represented by two C.P.A.'s prior to my coming into the case. Both of the C.P.A.'s backed out of the proceedings. I never did find out why, but my gut feeling is that they were afraid of losing their licenses. This case was one step away from being considered a criminal or tax fraud investigation. The C.P.A who prepared the return should have been found guilty of neglect. He backed out real quick. The second C.P.A. claimed to have a medical problem and could not proceed. I have my doubts about all of this, but I got the case, so here we go.

The taxpayers were very young. They had a good business in operation and were starting up another one. Although their records were in shambles, they did keep receipts and did their best to keep business and personal expenses separate. The tax years in question were 1993-1994-1995. I received the case in April of 1998.

The actual audit started in 1996 and had dragged on for two years before I came into the picture. A lot of damage was done in those two years. The young couple was accused of hiding income, so the audit turned into an "Economic Realty Audit". This type of audit assumes that taxpayers are making more money then they are reporting. To find out where the money is coming from, the i.r.s. looks into every phase of a person's lifestyle. They subpoenaed all bank accounts and property tax statements. They interviewed friends and associates. No stone was left unturned.

What this told me was that there had to be an i.r.s. informer. The original tax returns did not indicate anything except the taxpayers were not making a lot of money. They did report a profit for each of the tax years in question. When I questioned the i.r.s. about the possibility of an informer, they denied any knowledge of an informer.

In my forty years (at the time) of accounting and taxes I have never believed the i.r.s. and I was not about to start now. Something tipped the ice berg and It just bugged me no end. What in the world made them do such an extensive audit? After several weeks of thought, I finally figured it out.

The kids were buying a piece of land to build their dream house. They were making the lot payments in cash. This is what triggered the audit. Now my next question was how did the i.r.s. find out about the lot? There had to be an informer. I think I know who the informer was, but I could not make any comment during the audit. I still can't comment because I would be liable for slander.

Now that I had figured out the problem, I needed to find the solution. I knew that the kids got the money from relatives. The question was, how do we present the facts to the i.r.s.? I needed more time to see where the i.r.s. was coming from.

The total tax bill, including penalties, was $80,000 for the three year period. The i.r.s. denied the taxpayers all business deductions, plus they added outside income to justify their living expenses.

One item of Interest, to be inserted here, is that the i.r.s. has the authority to estimate living expenses for any taxpayer. They use

BLS, (Bureau Of Labor Statistics), numbers. Without going into a bunch of detail, the i.r.s. estimated these 22 year old kids needed an average of $30,000 extra money to live on. This was on top of the profit they reported on their tax returns. This put the taxpayers income in the $40,000 range. Now how many young couples, age 22, were making $40,000 in 1993?

When I read the audit papers, three things made the hair on the back of my neck stand up. First was the fact that two C.P.A.'s backed out of the case. Second, we have an i.r.s. auditor running up a tax bill on a taxpayer who has not been properly represented. Third was the fact that the i.r.s. added $30,000 a year to justify the taxpayers style of living which was not even close to being accurate.

After reviewing the audit papers and meeting with the clients, I decided to take on the case. I had just retired in October of the prior year, but this really intrigued me. Win, lose or draw, these young kids were going to be represented properly. Besides I knew I could whip the i.r.s. and this would be a good way to end my 43 years in the tax business, fighting the i.r.s. establishment.

By the time the case had come to me, the audit was closed out and the final assessment was made and ready to go to collections. Lucky for the taxpayers, they contacted me within the thirty day final notice period. This allowed us to file for an appeal and keep the audit active. Without seeing any numbers, I wrote a letter on behalf of the client stating a whole bunch of stuff that didn't even make sense to me, but it worked and we got an extension into Appeals.

I made six phone calls to the original auditor before he had the courtesy to get back to me. When we spoke, he was friendly, but did not offer anything. He told me my client was a liar and a cheat. I asked him if he looked at the clients receipts. He said my client did not have any receipts. I asked him if I could see the clients file. He told me that the file did not have anything that would help me, but he would give me some bank statements. He also told me that the case was out of his hands and he could not spend any more time on a dead issue. We agreed to meet in the lobby of the i.r.s. building and he would give me the bank statements.

I didn't really care what was in the clients file at this time. I knew I had the option to see the file, but I wanted the auditor to think I was just another dumb tax accountant. As long as I did not do, what the i.r.s. thought I should be doing, I had the upper hand. And, it worked.

In the chapter about choosing a tax preparer I mentioned that some preparers are licensed to practice before the i.r.s. and others are not. Well, I am not licensed anymore, because I'm retired. When the i.r.s. found out I was not licensed, they automatically assumed that I was not a qualified tax representative. This was my ace in the hole.

Because I was not licensed, I had to have the clients sign a power of attorney for me to represent them. When the auditor saw this power of attorney, he made several remarks about my representing the taxpayers. I learned more about this auditor in two phone calls, than I could have by reading his resume.

When I met the auditor in the lobby of the i.r.s. building I was not interested in what he gave me, but I wanted to read his personality. He was worse than I imagined. He was a smart alec, very smug and full of confidence. I was going to enjoy matching wits with this young pup.

As I have mentioned earlier, the i.r.s. is in no hurry to do anything. This was a great benefit to me and the clients. While the case was being shuffled about in the Appeals Division, we had time to study the client's records. I had a bookkeeper key punch every thing we had into an Excel program, which was summarized into a fairly decent profit and loss record. After I received all of the numbers in proper form, I saw immediately that the original C.P.A. had not done a good job at all.

About four months passed before the Appeals Division contacted us. I set up a meeting with an Appeals Officer to review my new findings. He reviewed the case and admitted the audit was not up to par. He agreed that if we had new evidence to prove our deductions, he would send the audit back to the field auditors for further review and negotiations.

He asked me if they could use the original i.r.s. auditor, because he was familiar with the case and could save a lot of time. Even though this seemed to be against all common sense in the tax world, I agreed. The auditor made a mess out of the last audit and I knew he would mess up again. The i.r.s. was falling right into the trap I was setting up for them.

The field auditor stopped by my office one afternoon to review the records. When he got there he spent about one hour asking me questions about 1996 information. I told him the audit was for the period 1993-1995 and 1996 had no bearing. He spent about ½ hour talking about my client being very evasive and not telling the truth.

He then spent about ½ hour talking about his golf game. Here is where he made the mistake I was looking for. His close golf buddy was the CPA who did the clients taxes. Bingo, I now knew who the informer was.

This CPA broke every rule of confidentiality. He should have lost his license and that is why he backed out of the case so quickly. Tax preparers have a very high ethics code which we all have to abide by. This CPA did just about everything wrong.

  The total time spent with the auditor was a little less than two hours. He did not ask one question about the records and receipts we were prepared to give him.

Then I told the auditor that the client had a bank account that I don't believe he had seen. He said that was not possible because he had subpoenaed all bank accounts. When I showed him the bank statements, he about died. Then I gave him a recap sheet which detailed various insurance company payments to the client for auto claims. These claims totaled about $15,000. He asked why the client did not deposit the claim monies. I told him I could not answer a personal question for the client.

Next, I gave him a complete new set of tax returns that I had prepared for the years 1993 - 1995 based on the records we had prepared. On these new tax returns, I included all insurance claim money that was business related, I included the sale of business assets and the additional income from the bank account no one knew about. I also included expenses that were paid out of the new account.

By the time I put everything together, the taxpayer's new returns showed very little difference in income than was reported on the original returns. However, all expenses and income were verified by the Excel sheets. The auditor still did not believe that the taxpayer had received the insurance money and did not make bank deposits.

Before he left I gave him our new Excel summary sheets. I told him I was moving to another part of the state and if possible I would like to do the audit by correspondence. Once we got to the end of his audit, I would come back to his office to negotiate the final outcome. He agreed. I also asked him if he wanted the clients receipts to verify the expenses. He said "No, these summary sheets and tax returns would do just fine".

After the auditor left, I prepared a summary of our meeting to give to the taxpayer. While I was typing up the summary my mind was going 100 miles an hour. Why didn't the auditor want to see receipts? Why did he talk about 1996 instead of the audit years? Why in the world did he come anyway? Then it dawned on me. He couldn't have cared less about the records. He was so sure that the client was a cheat, and that the informer's information would be all he needs.

Our meeting was in the middle of August. I moved to Northern California two weeks later. September came and went. Finally, I received his audit papers on October 13th. He made a few changes to my tax numbers, which I agreed to accept. He completely denied all auto expenses and all depreciation of trucks and other equipment. He also included his BLM figures as before, stating the insurance money and that of relatives was invalid.

I wrote back to the auditor stating our position on the auto and truck expenses. I listed in detail all cash money received by the taxpayers, including the dates received and where each dollar came from. I answered every position the auditor took, in detail and with proper verification. I mailed my answers on October 25th.

Sometime in November I received a new assessment for the three tax years totaling $50,000. I phoned the auditor immediately and asked how he could close out the audit without ever meeting with us. He again said that it was a dead issue and his supervisor told him to close out the case. He stated that the new assessment was lower by $30,000 and the taxpayer got off easy. The case was going back to Appeals Division.

Well folks, I was not a happy tax preparer. How could they get away with making some adjustments and then closing out the case without any personal contact? I wrote letters to the auditor, his supervisor and the Appeals Division Officer that I had contacted earlier.

I did not receive an answer from the auditor or his supervisor. I did receive a nice phone call from the Appeals Officer. He stated that it was not in his hands anymore, but that he would look into the matter and have someone contact me. Wow, a real person at the i.r.s.

I would like to state at this time that Appeals Officers are a different breed of cat from other auditors. Their job is to review cases in dispute and find an equitable solution. They are willing to give a taxpayer the benefit of doubt in almost every case. The Appeals Division is the last resort before the case goes to Tax Court. No one wants to go to court, not even the i.r.s.

The Appeals Officer phoned me in November 1998. I knew it was going to be a while before I heard from the Appeals Division. December, January, February and March passed and still no contact. Finally in April, I received a phone call from an Appeals Officer. She had been assigned the case and would need time to review the documents.

After a few weeks I received a letter from the Appeals Officer. I answered all of the questions the next day and fired off my answers. Two weeks later I received another phone call to set up a meeting with the taxpayers. I requested the meeting be on

Tuesday, May 18th. I did not want to meet with an auditor on Monday as it could be a very bad hair day for everyone.

I informed my clients of the meeting and then I got another surprise. They did not want to meet with the auditor. I assured them that this would be completely different than before. Not only would the atmosphere be different, but the Appeals Officer would be very polite and easy to work with. I also assured them that the case was going in our favor and that the tax bill would be very low, maybe a few thousand dollars at the most.

I met the client at a restaurant one hour before the scheduled meeting with the i.r.s. The wife did not come as the baby was sick. The client was scared to death. I spent the full hour calming him down and giving instructions on how to answer questions. He asked if the original auditor would be there. If he was, the client was going to walk out or punch him in the face. I told him that he would not be there and if he was, we had the option to ask him to leave.

I instructed the client to answer all questions truthfully and to keep the answers short. You never want to elaborate to an auditor. I told him that I was going to monitor the conversation and should he start to get himself in trouble I would bail him out. He seemed to feel better knowing that I was going to be watching the proceedings very carefully.

We met with the Appeals Officer at 10:00 am. She was a very nice, soft spoken person. The first thing she did was put the client at ease. After a little bit of chit chat she proceeded to ask questions. All of her questions were direct and short. The first ones were about the auto and truck expenses that had been denied. Next were questions about the land they were buying and where the money came from. After that, the questions were directed towards the taxpayers living habits. The interview was well planned.

My client opened up like a book. Much to the auditors surprise I let the client talk. He answered each question in detail and said some things I didn't even know. Every one of his answers were to his benefit, so I sat back and listened. Once in a while the auditor asked me if I had papers to support the answer and I would give

her what ever I had. This was the easiest audit I had ever done.
My client was doing all of the work for me.

The interview lasted about 2 hours and 15 minutes. At that time the
auditor got up and said she had heard all she needed and that she
would present her findings to us in a few days. We were out of
there.

When the client and I got outside of the building he turned to me
and said. "Gee, she was a nice person. Are all Appeals Officers
like that?" I just smiled.

The next question he asked was how did I think we did. I thought
we had done very well, but this is the i.r.s. and you never know
what to expect. My guess was that the tax bill could amount to a
few thousand dollars, which he should be prepared to pay. We
could go to tax court, but it would not be advisable. He agreed.

The meeting was on Tuesday morning. On Saturday of the same
week I received the revised audit figures and a tax bill. I
immediately phoned the client to see if they received the notice.
They did, but were afraid to open the envelope.

I played the notice up a bit to get them worried. I asked if they were
prepared to pay the assessment. I told them that I thought we had
done all we could and now it was time to pay. I kept rattling on and
on until he said a few explicit words and wanted to know the
damage. I finally told him that the tax bill had been reduced from
$80,000 down to $665.

There was a long silence at the other end of the phone. Then a
very weak voice came back and said "What happened to the
$80,000?" I told him that it just disappeared into thin air.

You have probably noticed that I did not go into a lot of detail about
how we whipped the i.r.s. First of all it would bore you to death and
second, my approach should be considered classified information.
Somewhere along the line i.r.s. auditors will read this book. I
certainly would not want any of them to know the various tricks
some accountants use to beat their system. The i.r.s. does not play

a fair game. There is only one set of rules and they write them. Some day all of this will change, but that may be a long way off.

The reason I added this audit to my book is to bring a very big inequity to your attention. What would have happened to these young taxpayers if I, or someone like me, did not come to their defense?

Well, this is what could have happened. The tax assessment would have gone on record. Since the taxpayers could not pay, the i.r.s. would foreclose on the kid's property and bank accounts. Next they would garnish the wages or any profits made through their efforts in the next ten years.

To offset this from happening, the kids would probably file for bankruptcy and eliminate the tax bill. By doing this the i.r.s. loses, the kids end up losing, and no one wins. All of this would happen because some stupid auditor had a bug up his rear and was probably trying to make a name for himself.

Speaking of the auditor, what ever happened to him? Was he fired, reprimanded or what? What about his supervisor? She approved everything he did and would not even consider the fact that maybe there was more to the audit than he produced. These two i.r.s. employees are a good example of what we have been reading about In the papers. They calculate large assessments against taxpayers during audits. This looks good on their records and gives them brownie points for bonuses or promotions.

If I was their boss and found out that an $80,000 tax assessment was reduced to $665, there would be some house cleaning going on real quick.

Over the years I have not seen very many happy endings to serious tax matters. I am very pleased that this case was resolved in a manner that benefited a very nice young couple. They now have faith in the system again and I hope they are able to get on with their lives. They sure deserve it.

GONE FISHING

Some Words Of Wisdom From The Author

Some Days you are the pigeon

And other days you are the statue

~~~~~~~~~~

Let your smile change the world

Don't let the world change your smile

ABOUT THE AUTHOR

Carey has been up and down "The Yellow Brick Road" so many times; he likens his life to a road map.

He has enjoyed every minute of the trip and wouldn't trade his experiences for anything.

Accomplishments

Carey is one of the largest joke book publishers on the internet

34 copyrights and 4 patent applications
Golfer for 78 years
Practicing tax accountant for 60 years
Bowling Professional for 30 years
Professional football handicapper, 28 years
Nevada Real Estate Broker 10 years
Owned and operated 27 businesses

Favorite Saying
If you keep on doing
What you have been doing,
You will keep on getting,
What you have been getting.
(Author Unknown)

~

Author's Favorite Thought
"Change is Inevitable"
~

Dedication
This book is dedicated to his two lovely daughters and their mother who have shared many of the trips along the way.

OTHER BOOKS BY THE AUTHOR

Non Fiction Books
BY Carey Erichson
Bowling Ages 7 to 70
Business is a Bitch
The Little Fish That Could
Fairy Tales From the I.R.S.
The Book Of Golf Tips
The Golf Shot Maker
The Rise & Fall of American Family Values
Remarry or Cohabitate

Joke Books By
Carey Erichson

Risque' Jokes Unlimited
I Laughed So Hard I Peed My Panties
Oppppsss I Peed My Panties Again
Jokes Grandma Shouldn't Hear
Grandpa's Naughty Joke Book
Mommy's Dirty Little Secrets
Grandma's Naughty Joke Book
Daddy's Dirty Little Joke Book
The Day My Private Part Died
Where Did My Virginity Go
Where Did My Willie Go
Naughty Jokes For Grown Ups
Risque' Water Cooler Jokes
Risque' Adult Joke Book

Let's Offend Everybody
Nice and Naughty Jokes
This Jokes On Me
These Jokes Are Great
What is A Selfie
Our 20th Joke Book
Man Rules vs Woman Rules
A Man's Fantasy
A Woman's Fantasy

www.http://kartines.com

Please visit our company website.
We sell the following items and services.

Golf Products
Bowling Products
Joke Books
Children Books
Golf Books
NFL Football Picks
NFL Football Stats
Disabled Walker Products
Income Tax Products

Or call us at:

209-295-7789